D0601291

Schwan's®
FAMILY FAVORITES
THE
BEST
OF THE ROUNDUP

__Schwan's Great Recipe Roundup Cookbook__ is the result of your overwhelming response to our request for your recipes using SCHWAN'S products as part of the ingredients. Narrowing down all the wonderful recipes we received so they would fit in this book was a difficult task. After extensive tasting and testing, we came up with a delightful variety of dishes we believe will make preparing your meals as much a pleasure as eating them. These and all the recipes we received show just how much thought and care you put on your table.

With today's hectic schedules, we know how difficult it can be to prepare nutritious, well-balanced and tasty meals. We also know that a balanced diet plays an important role in keeping you healthy and able to meet the demands on your time. The wide variety of appetizing and flavorful appetizers, snacks, beverages, soups, stews, salads, side dishes, main dishes, breads, jams, jellies and desserts in this cookbook will make nutritious eating fun.

At Schwan's we take our commitment to you seriously. Our goal is to provide a wide variety of foods you will be proud to put on your table and serve to your family and friends. We offer convenient products designed to go straight from your freezer into an oven or microwave and onto your table, as well as products that are delicious when prepared in a variety of creative ways.

These recipes will introduce you to many new and exciting ways to make our products into a pleasing complement to your meal. We hope you enjoy them.

Alfred Schwan

Chairman of the Board
& CEO

Consumer questions or comments? Please use our toll-free customer service number: 1-800-544-8708.
Book Design & Production: Tad Ware & Company, Inc. Photography: Tad Ware Photography

CONTENTS

Easy Elegance Orange Cream Pie p.165

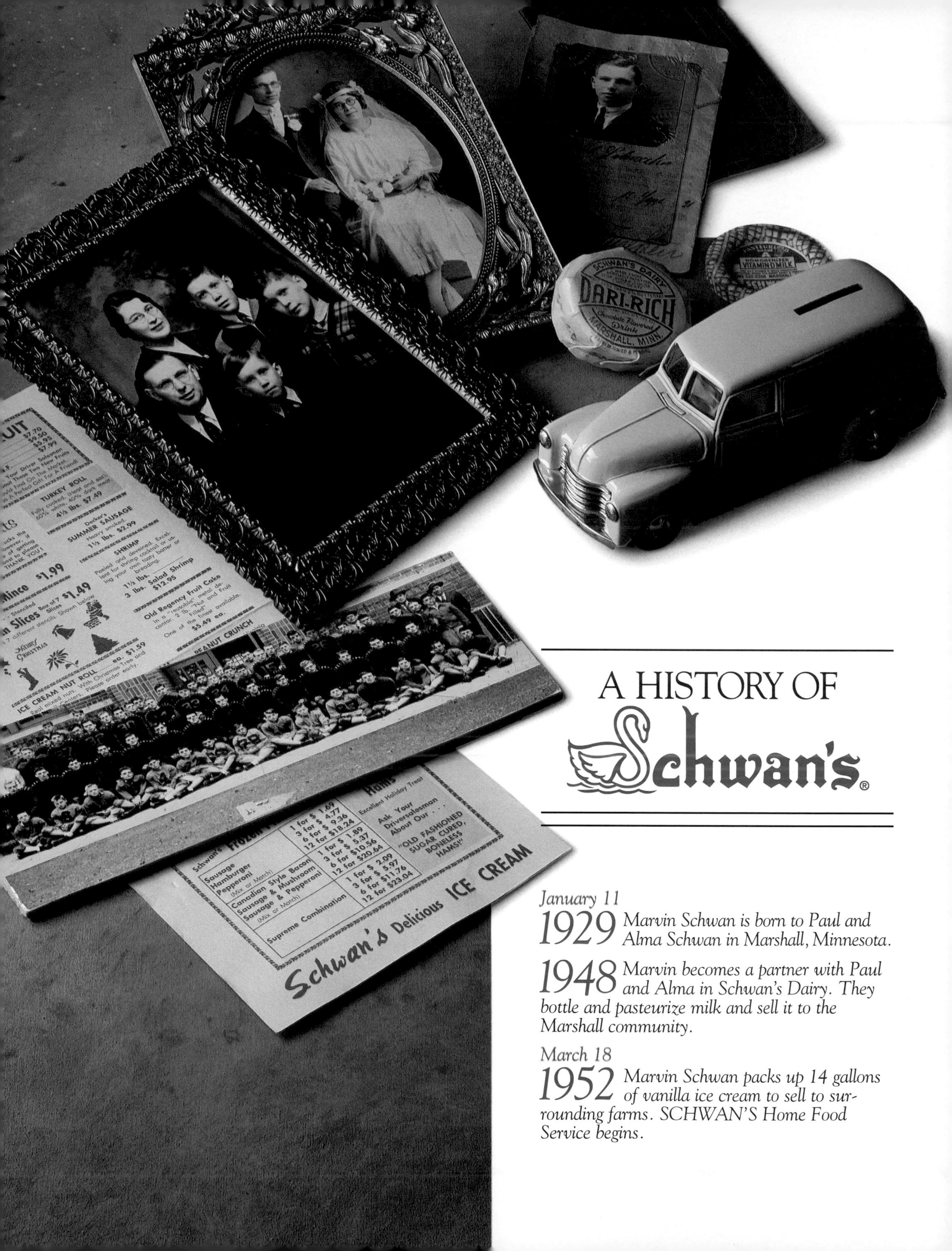

A HISTORY OF Schwan's®

January 11

1929 *Marvin Schwan is born to Paul and Alma Schwan in Marshall, Minnesota.*

1948 *Marvin becomes a partner with Paul and Alma in Schwan's Dairy. They bottle and pasteurize milk and sell it to the Marshall community.*

March 18

1952 *Marvin Schwan packs up 14 gallons of vanilla ice cream to sell to surrounding farms. SCHWAN'S Home Food Service begins.*

1954 *Marvin grows business to include six route men driving a fleet of five trucks.*

Marvin in front of an early route truck

1956 *First Schwan's outlying company depot is established in Sauk Centre, Minnesota.*

1957 *Grape, Orange, and Lemon Vita-Sun® Juice Drink Concentrate added to retail route system.*

Spring flood covers office and plant for four days.

The Marshall Flood of 1957 tests the young company

January
1964 *Alfred Schwan begins career at Schwan's Sales Enterprises.*

1965 *Schwan's purchases Vita-Sun® product line.*

1966 *First sale of frozen pizza is recorded off a Schwan's delivery truck.*

Ice Cream Plant begins production of ice cream sandwiches and drumsticks for sale on the route system.

1968 *The first seafood products (Haddock and Pollock) are introduced to the customers.*

February
1973 *BIG SAM steaks are introduced to Schwan's customers.*

July
1973 *Breaded Chicken Pieces are the first poultry item added to the route system.*

February 23
1974 *Fire destroys most of Marshall, Minnesota operation.*

Schwan's bounces back after $2 million fire

October 11
1974 *Marvin Schwan tells employees and local civic leaders,*

"We are going ahead with the distribution center in the Marshall Industrial Park. We will build an office complex on the ruins of the fire."

October
1976 *Schwan's produces its first Corn Dog. Corn Dogs are introduced nationwide in November, 1976.*

1978 *Schwan's first Mexican item, Burritos, is added to the route system.*

December
1985 *The first Oriental item, Pork Egg Rolls, is introduced to SCHWAN'S product line.*

Schwan's also introduces two Italian items, Beef Lasagna and Vegetable Lasagna.

1986 *Schwan's Ice Cream Plant is enlarged and moves to Industrial Park in Marshall.*

1987 *First Master Shopping Guide is published.*

First Master Shopping Guide

February
1989 *Frozen yogurt half gallons, in strawberry and peach flavors, is added to the route system.*

October
1994 *Schwan's Great Recipe Roundup begins.*

APPETIZERS, SNACKS & BEVERAGES

Start any party out right with these tasty tidbits and refreshing drinks. Some are hot, some are cold – all are delicious.

Broccoli Chicken Focaccia p.8

Broccoli Chicken Focaccia

$1,000 Winner
Diane Davidson, Texas

BROCCOLI CHICKEN FOCACCIA

"There are certain things that I keep on hand all the time, like Schwan's Stone Ground Wheat Bread Dough."
Diane Davidson

- **1 loaf SCHWAN'S Stone Ground Wheat Bread Dough, thawed and allowed to rise according to package directions**
- **¼ cup grated Parmesan cheese**
- **3 garlic cloves, finely minced**
- **1/16 to ⅛ teaspoon ground red pepper**
- **2 tablespoons olive oil**
- **3 thin slices red onion, separated into rings**
- **½ cup shredded mozzarella cheese**
- **4 GOURMET'S CHOICE Broccoli Spears, thawed, cut into 1-inch pieces**
- **⅔ cup SCHWAN'S Diced Chicken Meat**
- **½ cup shredded cheddar cheese**
- **Olive oil**

Heat oven to 375°F. Coat 13-inch to 15-inch pizza pan with olive oil. Pat bread dough into pan, forming raised edge. Bake at 375°F. for 15 minutes or until lightly browned.

Meanwhile, in small bowl, mix together Parmesan cheese, garlic and red pepper. Spread partially baked crust with 2 tablespoons olive oil and sprinkle with 3 tablespoons of Parmesan mixture. Top with onion rings, mozzarella cheese, broccoli, chicken, Cheddar cheese and remaining Parmesan mixture. Bake at 375°F. for 20 to 25 minutes or until heated through and cheese is melted. Refrigerate leftovers. 12 servings.

Schwan's TIP

Party Planning Tips

The secret to a successful party is all in the planning.

- Most importantly, give the kind of party you are most comfortable with.
- Consider space and time available to organize and prepare.
- Plan the theme and menu and send out invitations three to four weeks in advance.
- Select your recipes and make a list of ingredients to purchase.
- Decide on decorations, serving dishes and linens.
- Check around the house for "props" (baskets, crockery, lace, etc.) to use in creating an exciting atmosphere.

"*SCHWAN'S Home Food Service is convenient. They have really good quality products. It's nice to have someone come to your door.*"

Debbie Williams

Debbie Williams, Utah

HOT BREAD DIP

1 (1-lb.) round loaf sourdough bread, unsliced
3 (3-oz.) pkgs. cream cheese, softened
1½ cups dairy sour cream
1 tablespoon Worcestershire sauce
2 cups shredded Cheddar cheese
1 cup thinly sliced and chopped HAUGIN'S FARM BRAND Ham
¼ cup (½ can) diced green chilies
2 to 3 sliced green onions
½ teaspoon garlic salt
½ teaspoon seasoned salt
Assorted crackers, vegetable dippers or chips

Heat oven to 325°F. Cut 1-inch slice off top of loaf of bread; set aside. Scoop out bread, leaving a 1-inch shell; set bread shell and scooped-out bread aside. In medium bowl, beat together cream cheese, sour cream and Worcestershire sauce. Stir in cheese, ham, chilies, onions, garlic salt and seasoned salt; mix well. Spoon mixture into hollowed bread; replace top and wrap in foil.

Bake at 325°F. for 1 hour 30 minute to 2 hours or until dip is hot. Serve with pieces of scooped-out bread, crackers, vegetables and/or chips. 18 servings.

Linda Kosko, Pennsylvania

TASTY BAKED CHICKEN HORS D'OEUVRES

1 cup boiling water
1 chicken bouillon cube
5 SCHWAN'S Unbreaded Chicken Breast Filets, thawed
¼ cup lower-sodium soy sauce
3 tablespoons vinegar
2 tablespoons sugar
2 tablespoons brown sugar
1 teaspoon curry powder
Paprika
Black pepper
1½ cups GOURMET'S CHOICE Sugar Snap Peas
Blue cheese dressing, if desired

In 1-cup glass measuring cup, prepare chicken broth with boiling water and bouillon cube; set aside. Cut chicken into 1-inch cubes; set aside. In 13x9-inch or 11x7-inch pan, combine chicken broth, soy sauce, vinegar, sugar, brown sugar and curry powder; stir until well blended. Add chicken cubes; stir to coat with mixture and sprinkle lightly with paprika and pepper. Cover and refrigerate for 2 hours, stirring occasionally.

Heat oven to 325°F. Bake cubes in pan with marinade, uncovered, for 20 to 30 minutes or until chicken is no longer pink, basting frequently with cooking marinade. Add peas and bake 10 minutes longer. Arrange chicken cubes on serving dish with toothpicks; garnish with peas. Serve blue cheese dressing on the side, if desired. Refrigerate leftovers. 8 to 10 servings.

Betty Hook, New Hampshire

QUIK TATER® SKINS

45 GOURMET'S CHOICE QUIK TATERS
1 cup shredded sharp Cheddar cheese
2 slices HAUGIN'S FARM BRAND Thick Sliced Bacon, cooked and finely crumbled
1 to 2 tablespoons thinly sliced green onions
¼ to ⅓ cup dairy sour cream

Heat oven to 425°F. Lightly spray 10 to 12-inch pizza pan or cookie sheet with nonstick cooking spray. Arrange QUIK TATERS closely together in single layer in pan. Bake at 425°F. for 15 to 25 minutes or until light brown. Remove from oven; sprinkle with cheese, bacon and green onions. Continue baking for 5 minutes or until cheese is melted. Serve with sour cream on top or on the side. Refrigerate leftovers. 10 to 12 servings.

QUIK TATER Skins
Pineapple-Orange Delight *p.16*
Tasty Baked Chicken Hors d'oeuvres

Diane Enter, Wisconsin

REUBEN DIP

1 (15-oz.) tray LORI'S KITCHEN Creamed Chipped Beef, thawed
1 (14-oz.) can sauerkraut, drained
1 cup shredded Swiss cheese
½ cup Thousand Island dressing
Cocktail rye bread

In medium (2 to 2½-quart) microwave-safe dish, combine all ingredients *except* cocktail rye bread. Cover and microwave on HIGH for 8 minutes, stirring twice, until cheese is melted and dip is hot. Serve with cocktail rye bread. Refrigerate leftovers. 3¾ cups.

NOTE: Microwave timings are for 700 to 800 watt microwave ovens. With an oven of different wattage output, timings may need slight adjustment.

Brenda Heiberg, Wisconsin

CHICKEN & FETA CHEESE TRIANGLES

2 SCHWAN'S Unbreaded Chicken Breast Filets, thawed and chopped
1 (4-oz.) pkg. feta cheese with basil and tomato, crumbled
1 egg, lightly beaten
⅛ teaspoon freshly ground pepper
1 (8-oz.) pkg. refrigerated crescent rolls
Milk
2 teaspoons sesame seed

Cook chicken according to package directions; dice finely.

Heat oven to 375°F. In small bowl, combine chicken, cheese, egg and pepper; mix well. Unroll crescent rolls and separate into triangles. Press out triangles to enlarge slightly. Place 2½ tablespoons chicken mixture on center of each triangle Fold bottom two points of dough over filling. Fold top point of dough over filling and under dough; press all edges to seal, forming a triangle. Place on ungreased cookie sheet. Brush each triangle with milk and sprinkle with ¼ teaspoon sesame seeds. Repeat with remaining dough and filling. Bake at 375°F. for 10 to 18 minutes or until golden brown. Immediately remove from cookie sheet to serving dish. Refrigerate leftovers. 8 servings.

TIP: 1 (4-oz.) package plain feta cheese and 1 teaspoon dried basil leaves can be substituted for feta with tomato and basil.

The fleet's in! By 1955 SCHWAN'S Home Food Service was on the move as more salespeople and trucks are added to the fledgling company.

Cindy Pinkerton, Texas

CAJUN CHICKEN NIBBLES & CREOLE DIPPING SAUCE

CHICKEN NIBBLES

2 to 4 SCHWAN'S Unbreaded Chicken Breast Filets, cut into 1½-inch strips
½ teaspoon salt
¼ teaspoon cayenne pepper
¼ teaspoon black pepper
¼ teaspoon paprika
¼ teaspoon dried thyme leaves
⅛ teaspoon dried oregano leaves
⅛ teaspoon dried rosemary leaves

CREOLE DIPPING SAUCE

½ cup apricot preserves
1 to 4 teaspoons Creole mustard

In small bowl, combine all Chicken Nibbles ingredients, *except chicken;* sprinkle over chicken pieces and toss to coat. Refrigerate 10 minutes for chicken to absorb flavor. Sauté in hot oil until no longer pink, about 2 minutes. Keep warm while preparing Creole Dipping Sauce.

In small saucepan, over low heat, combine preserves and mustard; cook and stir until preserves are melted. Serve Chicken Nibbles with Creole Dipping Sauce. Refrigerate leftovers. 4 to 8 servings.

Jean Schilling, Tennessee

MARINATED POLISH SAUSAGE

6 to 8 links (1 to 1½ lbs.) HAUGIN'S PRIDE Polish Sausage, thawed, and sliced ½ to 1-inch thick
1 cup brandy or red cooking wine
2 tablespoons brown sugar
1 tablespoon dry mustard

In ½ gallon plastic freezer bag, place sausage slices. In small bowl, combine wine, sugar and mustard; pour into bag. Seal and refrigerate for 8 hours or overnight; turn bag occasionally.

Skillet Method: In large (12-inch) skillet over high heat, boil until most of the liquid has evaporated and sausage is brown, about 10 minutes.

Broiler Method: Heat broiler. Place sausage in 13x9-inch pan; broil 12 to 15 minutes or until sausage is brown, stirring every 3 minutes. Refrigerate leftovers.
8 to 12 servings.

Schwan's TIP

Q: How many party hors d'oeuvres should I plan for per person?

A: Amounts will vary depending on whether they will be followed by a meal, and if so, how closely. When no meal is planned, allow 10 to 12 per guest. If a meal follows closely, allow four or five per guest. If a late meal is planned, figure on six or seven per guest.

$5,000 Winner
Becky Danner, Ohio

STRAWBERRY TWISTERS

1½ cups GOURMET'S CHOICE Strawberries, frozen
½ cup water
½ cup rum
⅓ cup sugar
⅓ cup whipping cream
12 ice cubes
Whipping cream, whipped, or whipped topping
GOURMET'S CHOICE Strawberries

In blender container, combine all ingredients. Blend on high until ice cubes are crushed. Pour into glasses and top with whipped cream and a strawberry. 6 (5-oz.) servings.

"The Schwan's frozen Strawberries I use in my Strawberry Twisters are big, red and ripe all year round."

Becky Danner

Strawberry Twisters

PANSY

Betsy Morales, Pennsylvania

PINEAPPLE-ORANGE DELIGHT

4 cups boiling water
8 blackberry flavored tea bags
⅔ cup sugar
5 cups prepared VITA-SUN Pineapple Orange Juice Drink

In medium saucepan, pour water over tea bags; steep for 5 minutes. Remove tea bags. Stir in sugar and chill. Stir in juice. Store in refrigerator or freezer. 8 (8-oz.) servings.

Barbara Beyer, Michigan

BLACK RASPBERRY COCKTAIL

1 (8-oz) carton VITA-SUN Black Raspberry Juice Drink Concentrate
4 cups ginger ale, chilled
2 cups water
2 tablespoons honey
2 teaspoons cooking sherry or sherry wine

In 2-quart shaker, combine all ingredients; shake gently. Pour over ice to serve. 9 (6-oz.) servings.

You don't need a special holiday or occasion to enjoy SCHWAN'S ice cream, but it certainly is a good excuse – as this 1950's ad suggests.

Deborah White, Washington

PEANUT BUTTER POPCORN

1/3 cup peanut butter
1 tablespoon honey
1 tablespoon butter
4 cups popped GOURMET'S CHOICE Microwave Popcorn or GOURMET'S CHOICE Natural Lite Microwave Popcorn

In 1-cup glass measuring cup, mix peanut butter, honey and butter; microwave on high for 30 seconds, or until ingredients are melted, stirring to blend. In large (3 to 4-quart) bowl, place popped popcorn; pour peanut butter mixture over and stir until well coated. Refrigerate at least 30 minutes before serving. Store, covered, in the refrigerator. 4 cups.

NOTE: Microwave timings are for 700 to 800 watt microwave ovens. With an oven of different wattage output, timings may need slight adjustment.

Schwan's TIP

Q: What makes popcorn "pop"?

A: As the kernel is heated, the moisture inside changes to steam. The hard outer surface resists the building pressure until it finally bursts. The soft starch inside pops out as the steam inside the kernel is released and the kernel turns inside out.

Sharon Heurung, Minnesota

SCHWAN'S "SUPER BOWL" SNACK

2 (3.5-oz.) bags GOURMET'S CHOICE Microwave Popcorn or GOURMET'S CHOICE Natural Lite Microwave Popcorn, popped
2 (1 3/4-oz.) cans shoestring potatoes
1 cup salted mixed nuts
1/4 cup butter or margarine, melted
1 teaspoon dill weed
1 teaspoon Worcestershire sauce
1/2 teaspoon lemon pepper seasoning
1/4 teaspoon garlic powder
1/4 teaspoon onion powder

Heat oven to 325°F. In roasting pan, combine popcorn, potatoes and nuts. In small bowl, combine butter, dill weed, Worcestershire sauce, lemon pepper, garlic powder and onion powder; mix well. Pour over popcorn mixture; mix well until evenly coated. Bake at 325°F. for 8 to 10 minutes. Cool completely; store in tightly covered containers. 16 cups.

TIP: Mixture may be divided in half and baked in two 13x9-inch pans. Bake as directed.

Janelle Evert, Minnesota

FRUIT SLUSH

3 cups water
2 cups sugar
4 (8-oz.) cartons VITA-SUN Pineapple Orange Juice Drink Concentrate
2 (8-oz.) cartons SCHWAN'S Orange Juice Concentrate
1 (8-oz.) carton SCHWAN'S Lemonade Concentrate
4 cups GOURMET'S CHOICE Strawberries, thawed
3 bananas
Lemon-lime soda, chilled

In large saucepan, boil water and sugar until sugar is dissolved; cool. Add juice concentrates; set aside. In blender container, process strawberries until smooth; add to juice mixture in saucepan. Then process bananas; add to juice mixture. Using wire whisk, mix well. Place in covered freezer container; freeze. To serve, place 1 scoop (½ cup) into serving glass and fill with lemon-lime soda. 28 (4-oz.) servings.

Amy Daniels, Ohio

FRUIT FREEZE

1½ cups prepared VITA-SUN Orange Juice Drink
1 banana
½ cup GOURMET'S CHOICE Sliced Peaches
½ cup GOURMET'S CHOICE Strawberries
2 ice cubes

In blender container, combine all ingredients. Process all ingredients until smooth. 6 (4-oz.) servings.

Clockwise from top:
Fruit Slush
Berry Froth p.20
Fruit Freeze

Schwan's TIP

Q: Can I double or triple my recipes to get more servings?

A: It is best to make several batches of the same recipe. Some recipes, especially ones for baked goods, do not work well when they are increased.

Vicky Patoine, New York

BERRY FROTH

2 cups SCHWAN'S Rainbow Sherbet, softened
1½ cups prepared SCHWAN'S Pink Grapefruit Juice Cocktail
1 cup frozen raspberries, thawed, or 1 cup fresh raspberries.

In blender container, combine all ingredients. Process all ingredients until smooth. 6 (4-oz.) servings.

Corrine Hilsgon, Minnesota

ORANGE-PINEAPPLE SLUSH

2 (46-oz.) cans pineapple juice
1 (8-oz.) carton prepared SCHWAN'S Orange Juice
2 cups piña colada mix
½ cup grenadine syrup
Lemon-lime soda, chilled

In 2½-quart freezer container, combine all ingredients; mix well. Freeze. One hour before serving, remove frozen mixture from freezer; let stand at room temperature. To serve, spoon into glasses; fill with lemon-lime soda and stir. 38 (8-oz.) servings.

VARIATION: Can add 1 tablespoon rum to each glass before serving.

A collection of VITA-SUN juice drink concentrate bottles from the 50's and 60's.

Janet Banks, Texas

PUMPKIN PARTY PUNCH

6 cups prepared VITA-SUN Apple Juice Drink
1 (30-oz.) can pumpkin pie mix
4 cups SCHWAN'S Premium Vanilla Ice Cream
1 liter lemon-lime soda, chilled

In large bowl, combine apple juice and pumpkin pie mix; chill. In large punch bowl, just before serving, combine pumpkin mixture and ice cream; stir until smooth. Gently stir in soda. 32 (4-oz.) servings.

Terri Fargason, Texas

HOT SPICED TEA

1 tablespoon whole cloves
4 cinnamon sticks
1 (7.5-oz.) carton SCHWAN'S Tea Concentrate, thawed
Water
½ cup SCHWAN'S Orange Juice Concentrate, thawed
¼ cup SCHWAN'S Lemonade Concentrate, thawed
⅓ cup red hot cinnamon candies
¼ cup firmly packed brown sugar
⅛ teaspoon salt

Place cloves and cinnamon sticks in spice bag or cheese cloth; set aside. Prepare tea according to package directions. In large saucepan, combine prepared tea, spice bag, orange juice and lemonade concentrates, candies, brown sugar and salt; bring to a boil, stirring until candies dissolve. Reduce heat; simmer 5 minutes. Remove spice bag. Serve hot. 10 (6-oz.) servings.

"Rich and creamy" gives SCHWAN'S ice cream that "old-fashioned" flavor. This particular advertisement said that and more in 1953.

SOUPS, STEWS & SALADS

From hearty, warming soups and chowders to crunchy and colorful salads, this chapter is full of light and easy lunch ideas and great first courses.

Clockwise from top left:
Tortilla Soup p.26
Italian Chicken Soup p.25
Tortellini Soup p.24

Tortellini Soup

$1,000 Winner
William Klein, New Mexico

TORTELLINI SOUP

"My in-laws were using Schwan's and we started getting it because we liked it a lot."

William Klein

- **2 teaspoons oil**
- **1 tablespoon dried basil leaves**
- **2 garlic cloves, minced**
- **4 cups chicken broth**
- **1½ cups LORI'S KITCHEN Chicken Tortellini or Cheese Tortellini**
- **¼ teaspoon salt**
- **⅛ teaspoon pepper**
- **1 (14½-oz.) can diced tomatoes**
- **1 cup GOURMET'S CHOICE Cut Green Beans**
- **1 cup GOURMET'S CHOICE California Blend**

Heat oil in large saucepan over medium-high heat. Add basil and garlic; cook 1 minute, stirring constantly. Add broth, tortellini, salt and pepper; bring to a boil. Reduce heat to medium. Cover; simmer 10 minutes. Add tomatoes, green beans and California Blend; bring to a boil. Reduce heat to medium-low. Cover; simmer 10 minutes. Refrigerate leftovers. 8 (1¼-cup) servings.

$1,000 Winner
Peggy Burns, Arkansas

ITALIAN CHICKEN SOUP

2 teaspoons olive oil
4 SCHWAN'S Unbreaded Chicken Breast Filets, cut into 1-inch pieces
½ cup (1 stalk) chopped celery
½ cup (1 medium) chopped onions
2 garlic cloves, minced
1 teaspoon dried basil leaves
1 teaspoon Italian herb seasoning*
¼ teaspoon pepper
2 cups water
3 chicken bouillon cubes
1 (14½-oz.) can tomatoes, undrained
1 cup GOURMET'S CHOICE Cut Leaf Spinach
1 ounce uncooked vermicelli, broken into 2-inch pieces
Grated Parmesan cheese

Heat oil in large saucepan or Dutch oven. Add chicken pieces. Cook over medium-high heat 4 to 6 minutes, or until lightly browned, stirring occasionally. Add celery, onions and garlic; cook 3 to 5 minutes, or until vegetables are crisply tender. Stir in basil, Italian seasoning, pepper, water, bouillon cubes and tomatoes with liquid; bring to a boil. Reduce heat to medium. Cover; simmer 5 minutes. Stir in spinach and vermicelli. Cover; simmer 10 minutes or until thoroughly heated and vermicelli is tender. Sprinkle servings with grated Parmesan cheese. Refrigerate leftovers.
6 (1-cup) servings.

TIPS: 2 cups SCHWAN'S Diced Chicken Meat can be substituted for the 4 SCHWAN'S Unbreaded Chicken Breast Filets.

*¼ teaspoon each dried oregano leaves, dried marjoram leaves and dried basil leaves and ⅛ teaspoon rubbed dried sage can be substituted for 1 teaspoon Italian herb seasoning.

"Schwan's plays a large part in planning our meals. My husband and I are weight watchers. We do a lot with the nonfat ice cream products and we really like the frozen vegetables."

Peggy Burns

$1,000 Winner
Martha Snyder, Texas

TORTILLA SOUP

- 1 cup SCHWAN'S Diced Chicken Meat
- 2 (14½-oz.) cans chicken broth
- 1 (14½-oz.) can diced tomatoes with chilies, undrained
- 1 (15-oz.) can kidney beans, drained, rinsed
- ½ cup GOURMET'S CHOICE Cut Corn
- ½ cup GOURMET'S CHOICE Cut Green Beans
- ½ cup GOURMET'S CHOICE Baby Carrots, slightly thawed and diced
- 2 tablespoons dry taco seasoning mix
- 2 cups water
- 2 cups broken tortilla chips
- ½ cup shredded mozzarella cheese

In large saucepan or Dutch oven, combine chicken, broth, tomatoes with chilies, kidney beans, corn, beans, carrots, taco seasoning and water; mix well. Bring to a boil over medium-high heat. Reduce heat to medium; cook 45 to 60 minutes to blend flavors. To serve, ladle soup into bowls and top with chips and cheese. Serve immediately. Refrigerate leftovers. 6 (1½-cup) servings.

"We started using the Schwan's service because of the quality of products and the convenience of having them delivered to the house."

Martha Snyder

Neva Thomas, Virginia

TORTELLINI MINESTRONE

- 1 tablespoon olive oil
- 1 cup (1 large) chopped onions
- 1 pound HAUGIN'S PRIDE Polish Sausage, cut into ⅛-inch slices
- 1 (16½-oz.) can whole tomatoes, chopped
- 4 cups chicken broth
- 2 cups water
- 1 cup (2 stalks) celery
- 1 cup light red kidney beans, drained and rinsed
- 1 cup GOURMET'S CHOICE Cut Green Beans
- ½ cup GOURMET'S CHOICE Cut Corn
- 1 teaspoon dried oregano leaves
- ½ teaspoon garlic powder
- 2 cups LORI'S KITCHEN Chicken Tortellini

Heat olive oil in large saucepan or Dutch oven. Sauté onions over medium-high heat 3 to 5 minutes, or until tender, stirring occasionally. Add sausage; cook until lightly browned. Add tomatoes, broth, water, celery, kidney beans, green beans, corn, oregano and garlic powder; mix well. Bring to a boil. Add tortellini; reduce heat to medium. Cook for 35 minutes, stirring occasionally. Refrigerate leftovers. 8 (1½-cup) servings.

Sandra Niederhofer, New York

SPINACH & TORTELLINI SOUP

- 2 tablespoons butter or margarine
- ½ cup (1 medium) finely chopped onions
- ½ cup (1 stalk) finely chopped celery
- ¼ cup grated carrots
- 3½ cups chicken broth
- 1 (1½ lb.) package LORI'S KITCHEN Chicken Tortellini or Cheese Tortellini
- 1 cup chopped fresh mushrooms
- 3 cups GOURMET'S CHOICE Cut Leaf Spinach, thawed, drained, chopped
- ¼ teaspoon dried basil leaves
- ⅛ teaspoon pepper
- ⅛ teaspoon dried thyme leaves
- 1 cup half and half, whole milk or 2% milk
- Salt, to taste

Melt butter in large saucepan over medium-high heat. Sauté onions, celery and carrots 3 to 5 minutes until tender, stirring occasionally. Add broth. Bring to a boil; add tortellini and mushrooms. Reduce heat to medium; cook 5 to 10 minutes, or until tortellini is tender, stirring occasionally. Stir in spinach, basil, pepper, thyme, milk and salt. Cook 2 minutes, stirring occasionally. Refrigerate leftovers. 8 (1-cup) servings.

Jeanette Gigvere, Connecticut

HEARTY CHICKEN SOUP

- 8 cups water
- 1 cup uncooked wide egg noodles
- 2 cups GOURMET'S CHOICE Stir-Fry Vegetables
- 4 tablespoons chicken bouillon granules
- 2 tablespoons chopped fresh parsley OR 1 tablespoon dried parsley flakes
- 2 cups SCHWAN'S Diced Chicken Meat
- Salt
- Pepper

In large saucepan or Dutch oven over medium-high heat, bring water to a boil. Add noodles, vegetables, bouillon and parsley. Bring to a boil, stirring occasionally. Cover; reduce heat to medium. Cook 10 minutes, or until noodles are tender. Add chicken. Cover; turn off heat. Let stand 10 minutes. Salt and pepper to taste. Refrigerate leftovers. 10 (1-cup) servings.

Schwan's TIP

Healthy Soup Tips

- Reduce fat and calories in homemade soups.
- Instead of thickening soups with a fat and flour roux, puree one or more of the vegetables and return the puree to the soup. Instant mashed potato flakes also work well.
- To remove excess fat from soup, cover and chill it overnight or until the fat solidifies on the surface of the soup. Then lift off the fat and discard it.

Linda Jasso, Michigan

FISH CHOWDER

- 4 SEAFARER'S CHOICE Orange Roughy Fillets, slightly thawed and cut into bite-sized pieces
- 4 (16-oz.) cans stewed tomatoes
- 2 cups SEAFARER'S CHOICE P & D Shrimp
- 1 (6.5 oz.) can minced clams, undrained
- 1½ cups (3 stalks) diced celery
- ¼ teaspoon white pepper
- 1 cup GOURMET'S CHOICE Cut Corn
- 1 tablespoon dried oregano leaves
- 2 teaspoons dried rosemary leaves

In slow cooker, combine all ingredients; mix well. Cover; cook on LOW for 6 to 8 hours. Refrigerate leftovers. 10 (1¼-cup) servings.

TIP: Fish chowder can be prepared on the stove. In large saucepan or Dutch oven, combine all ingredients; mix well. Cover; cook over medium heat 1½ to 2 hours or until heated through, stirring occasionally.

Schwan's TIP

Q: Can milk be substituted for half and half?

A: When you are making a cooked product, substitute 1 tablespoon melted butter plus enough whole milk to make 1 cup.

Debbie Sherbahn, Kentucky

SEAFOOD CHOWDER

- ½ cup GOURMET'S CHOICE Baby Carrots
- 3 to 4 large potatoes, cut into 1-inch pieces
- ½ pound SEAFARER'S CHOICE Cod Fillets
- 1 cup margarine or butter
- 1 cup all-purpose flour
- 2 (14½-oz.) cans chicken broth
- 4 cups half and half
- ½ pound SEAFARER'S CHOICE P & D Shrimp, cooked and cut into small pieces
- ⅛ teaspoon salt
- ¼ teaspoon pepper

In medium saucepan, cook carrots and potatoes in enough water to cover for 8 to 10 minutes, or until tender. Add cod. Cook 5 minutes; drain. Set aside.

Melt margarine in large saucepan or Dutch oven over medium heat. Add flour; cook 1 minute, stirring constantly. Stir in chicken broth and half and half. Cook 5 to 10 minutes or until mixture is hot, stirring occasionally. Add potatoes, carrots, cod, shrimp, salt and pepper. Reduce heat to low; cook for 10 to 20 minutes or until thickened and hot, stirring frequently. Refrigerate leftovers. 12 (1-cup) servings.

Fish Chowder (top)
Seafood Chowder (bottom)

Madelen Rowe, Idaho

CORN CHOWDER

2 tablespoons butter or margarine
1 cup (1 large) chopped onions
½ cup (1 stalk) minced celery
1 green bell pepper, minced
4 cups GOURMET'S CHOICE Cut Corn
½ teaspoon salt
½ teaspoon dried basil leaves
¼ teaspoon dried thyme leaves
1 cup vegetable broth, chicken broth or water
1 cup evaporated milk

Melt butter in large saucepan over medium-high heat. Add onions. Cook and stir 3 to 5 minutes. Add celery; continue cooking for 5 minutes. Stir in green pepper, corn, salt, basil and thyme. Cover; reduce heat to medium. Cook for 5 minutes, stirring occasionally. Stir in broth; mix well. Cover; simmer 10 minutes. In food processor blender container, pureé about 2¾ cups (about half of the mixture) until smooth. Pour pureé mixture into remaining corn mixture. Cook over medium heat 5 to 10 minutes, or until heated through, stirring occasionally. Just before serving, stir in evaporated milk. Cook over low heat until heated through, stirring frequently. Refrigerate leftovers. 6 (1-cup) servings.

Margaret Howard, Texas

SEAFOOD MUSHROOM CHOWDER

2 tablespoons oil
¼ cup diced onions
¼ cup diced green bell pepper
1 pound SEAFARER'S CHOICE IQF Ocean Perch, Blue Hake Prime Cut Loins or IQF Cod Fillets, slightly thawed and cubed
1 pound GOURMET'S CHOICE Early Garden Blend, thawed
1 pound SEAFARER'S CHOICE P & D Shrimp
1 (10⅔-oz.) can chicken broth
1 (8-oz.) can potatoes, drained and cubed
1 (6-oz.) can sliced mushrooms, undrained
1¼ cups water
1 teaspoon salt
⅛ teaspoon dried thyme leaves
½ cup half and half or evaporated milk
2 tablespoons cornstarch

Heat oil in large saucepan or Dutch oven over medium-high heat. Sauté onions and green pepper 3 to 5 minutes, or until tender. Add fish, vegetables, shrimp, chicken broth, potatoes, mushrooms, water, salt and thyme. Bring to a boil. Cover; reduce heat to low. Cook 15 minutes, stirring occasionally. In small bowl, combine half and half with cornstarch; mix well. Stir into chowder. Cook, stirring constantly, over low heat for 5 to 8 minutes, or until thickened. Refrigerate leftovers. 8 (1-cup) servings.

Norma Zinsmeyer, Texas

EASY GULF COAST GUMBO

- 1/4 cup oil
- 1 1/2 cups (3 stalks) diced celery
- 1 diced green bell pepper
- 5 cups water
- 4 chicken bouillon cubes
- 1 teaspoon gumbo filé
- 1 teaspoon dried basil leaves
- 1/4 teaspoon garlic salt
- 1/4 teaspoon onion salt
- 1/4 teaspoon celery salt
- 1 bay leaf
- 1 pound SEAFARER'S CHOICE Ocean Perch IQF, cut into 1-inch pieces
- 1 pound SEAFARER'S CHOICE P & D Shrimp
- 1 (6.5-oz.) can chopped clams
- 1 pint oysters, if desired
- 1 cup okra, if desired
- Salt, to taste
- Pepper, to taste

Heat oil in large saucepan over medium-high heat. Add green pepper and celery. Sauté over medium-high heat 3 to 5 minutes, or until tender. Reduce heat to low. Add water, bouillon cubes, gumbo filé, basil, garlic salt, onion salt, celery salt and bay leaf. Cook, uncovered, for 1 1/4 hours, stirring occasionally.

Add fish, shrimp, clams, oysters, okra and salt and pepper to taste. Continue cooking for 15 minutes. Refrigerate leftovers. 9 (1-cup) servings.

Bernice Smith, Oklahoma

JAMBALAYA

- 1/4 cup butter or margarine
- 1 cup (1 large) chopped onions
- 1/2 small green bell pepper, cut into strips
- 1 garlic clove, crushed
- 1/4 teaspoon chili powder
- 1/4 teaspoon cumin
- 4 cups cooked GOURMET'S CHOICE IQF White Rice
- 2 cups SEAFARER'S CHOICE P & D Shrimp, cooked
- 1 cup HAUGIN'S FARM BRAND Ham, cut into strips
- 2 cups tomato juice
- 1 cup small whole ripe pitted olives
- 3 drops hot pepper sauce
- 2 teaspoons chopped fresh parsley

Melt butter in large saucepan or Dutch oven over medium-high heat; sauté onions, green pepper, garlic, chili powder and cumin 3 to 5 minutes, or until onions and green pepper are tender. Add remaining ingredients *except* parsley; mix well. Cover; cook 8 to 10 minutes or until thoroughly heated. Just before serving, sprinkle with parsley. Refrigerate leftovers. 9 (1-cup) servings.

Kathy Boeser, Minnesota

CHICKEN CHILI

1 tablespoon oil
2 garlic cloves, minced
1 cup (1 large) chopped onions
1 teaspoon ground cumin
3 cups SCHWAN'S Diced Chicken Meat
2 cups cooked GOURMET'S CHOICE IQF White Rice
1 (16-oz.) can white kidney (cannellini) beans, drained and rinsed
2 (4-oz.) cans diced green chilies, undrained
1 cup GOURMET'S CHOICE Cut Corn
½ teaspoon hot pepper sauce
Shredded Colby-Jack cheese

Heat oil in large saucepan or Dutch oven; sauté garlic and onions 3 to 5 minutes, or until tender, stirring occasionally. Stir in cumin, chicken, rice, kidney beans, chilies and corn. Reduce heat to medium; cook 25 to 30 minutes, or until thoroughly heated, stirring occasionally. Add hot pepper sauce. Serve topped with shredded cheese, if desired. Refrigerate leftovers. 10 (1-cup) servings.

Marvin Schwan ventured into the food business by helping his parents in their dairy and lunch business. Here are two ad signs from 1943.

Ruth Smith, Michigan

NO-FAT TURKEY CHILI

4 LORI'S KITCHEN Unbreaded Turkey Breast Filets, cut into 1-inch pieces
2 (15-oz.) cans Great Northern Beans, drained and rinsed
1 (15-oz.) can black beans, drained and rinsed
1 (15-oz.) can red kidney beans, drained and rinsed
2 cups salsa
1 (15-oz.) can tomato sauce
½ teaspoon salt, optional
⅛ teaspoon pepper

In large saucepan or Dutch oven over medium heat, cook turkey 5 to 7 minutes or until lightly browned. Stir in all remaining ingredients; mix well. Bring to a boil over medium-high heat. Reduce heat to medium; cook 25 to 30 minutes to blend flavors, stirring occasionally. Refrigerate leftovers. 10 (1-cup) servings.

Schwan's TIP

Q: Can fresh herbs be substituted for dried herbs?

A: Yes. Just triple the amount of dried leaf herb called for in the recipe. Do the reverse when you're substituting a dried leaf herb for fresh because dried herbs have a more concentrated flavor. When you're substituting ground herbs for dried leaf herbs, use about half the amount called for.

Meta Plevnic, Texas

POTATO, CABBAGE POTAGE

5 cups (5 medium) potatoes, peeled and diced
½ cup (1 medium) chopped onions
½ cup water
5 slices HAUGIN'S FARM BRAND Thick Sliced Bacon, diced and fried crisp
2 HAUGIN'S PRIDE Polish Sausages, sliced and browned
2 cups milk
8 slices SCHWAN'S American Processed Cheese, cut into fourths
¼ head (about 2 cups) cabbage, chopped fine
Salt, to taste
Pepper, to taste

In large saucepan or Dutch oven, combine potatoes and onions. Add enough water to cover vegetables. Bring to a boil over medium-high heat, stirring occasionally. Reduce heat to medium. Cover; cook 20 to 30 minutes until vegetables are very tender and water is thick, stirring occasionally. Add remaining ingredients. Cook 15 to 18 minutes, or until cabbage is crisp-tender and cheese is melted. Add salt and pepper to taste. Refrigerate leftovers. 9 (1-cup) servings.

TIP: Serve hot with LORI'S KITCHEN 5-Cheese Garlic French Bread

Debra Smith, Illinois

QUICK & DELICIOUS VEGETABLE BEEF SOUP

1 tablespoon oil
3 HAUGIN'S PRIDE Sirloin Ball Tip Steaks, cut into bite-sized pieces
½ cup (1 medium) chopped onions
½ cup (1 stalk) thinly sliced celery
5 cups tomato juice
1 cup GOURMET'S CHOICE Cut Corn
1 cup GOURMET'S CHOICE Green Peas
1 cup GOURMET'S CHOICE Baby Carrots
½ cup quick pearled barley
½ teaspoon salt, if desired
⅛ teaspoon pepper

Heat oil in Dutch oven over medium-high heat. Add steak pieces, onions and celery. Cook 5 to 6 minutes or until steak is browned, stirring occasionally. Add tomato juice; bring to a boil. Reduce heat to medium; cook for 25 to 30 minutes, or until beef is tender, stirring occasionally. Add corn, peas and carrots; cook 15 minutes, or until vegetables are tender. Stir in barley, salt and pepper. Cover; cook for 10 minutes, or until barley is tender, stirring occasionally. Additional tomato juice can be added if soup becomes too thick. Refrigerate leftovers. 6 (1⅓-cup) servings.

TIP: Serve with warm SCHWAN'S Stone Ground Wheat Bread or White Bread.

Neva Thomas, Virginia

VEGETABLE STEW & COUSCOUS

1 tablespoon olive oil
1 large onion, thinly sliced
3 garlic cloves, minced
1 (16-oz.) can chick peas (garbanzo beans), drained and rinsed
4 cups chicken broth, divided
1 cup water
½ teaspoon dried thyme leaves
½ teaspoon dried basil leaves
½ teaspoon dried marjoram leaves
1 large bay leaf
3 cups GOURMET'S CHOICE California Blend
1 medium yellow summer squash, cubed
1 (15-oz.) can stewed tomatoes
½ teaspoon salt
¼ teaspoon pepper
2 cups GOURMET'S CHOICE Sugar Snap Peas
3 tablespoons raisins
1½ cups couscous

Heat oil in large saucepan or Dutch oven over medium-high heat. Add onions; sauté 3 to 5 minutes until tender, stirring occasionally. Add garlic; cook 1 minute. Stir in chick peas, 2½ cups of the broth, water, thyme, basil, marjoram and bay leaf. Bring to a gentle boil. Reduce heat to medium; boil gently for 6 to 8 minutes. Remove bay leaf. Add California Blend, squash, tomatoes, salt and pepper. Cook for 15 to 20 minutes, stirring occasionally. Stir in sugar snap peas. Cover; turn off heat. Let stand for 10 to 12 minutes.

Meanwhile, in small saucepan over medium-high heat, bring the remaining 1½ cups of broth and the raisins to full boil. Add couscous. Cover; remove from heat. Let stand 10 minutes or until liquid is absorbed. Fluff couscous with a fork. Serve vegetables over couscous. Refrigerate leftovers.
8 (1½-cup) servings.

Vegetable Stew & Couscous p.35

Patsy White, Georgia

INSTANT BRUNSWICK STEW

1 (1½-lb.) package HAUGIN'S PRIDE Chopped BBQ Beef with Sauce
1 (1-lb.) package SCHWAN'S Chicken Breast Meat for Fajitas, chopped
3 cups GOURMET'S CHOICE Cut Corn
1 (9-oz.) box frozen lima beans
1 (16-oz.) can tomato pureé
½ cup (1 medium) chopped onions
1 tablespoon vinegar
1 tablespoon lemon juice
1 tablespoon Worcestershire sauce
2 teaspoons salt
1 teaspoon pepper

In large saucepan or Dutch oven, combine all ingredients; mix well. Cook, uncovered, over medium heat 20 to 25 minutes or until thoroughly heated, stirring occasionally. Refrigerate leftovers. 9 (1-cup) servings.

Diann Zentner, Louisiana

CHICKEN SALAD

SALAD
2 cups (12 oz.) SCHWAN'S Diced Chicken Meat
2 cups (about ½) honeydew melon, cut into 1-inch cubes
½ cup GOURMET'S CHOICE Strawberries, halved, thawed and well drained
½ cup slivered almonds

DRESSING
½ cup mayonnaise
½ teaspoon curry powder

In large bowl, combine all salad ingredients; toss gently. In small bowl, combine all dressing ingredients; mix well. Pour dressing over salad; toss gently to coat. Cover; refrigerate at least 2 hours to blend flavors. Refrigerate leftovers. 5 (1-cup) servings.

Schwan's TIP

Hints for Great Tasting Salads

- Clean and chill ingredients ahead of time. Also chill salad plates and bowls.
- If a salad includes tomatoes, add them just before tossing to keep them from diluting the dressing.
- Mix a tossed salad with its dressing at the last minute to prevent the dressing from wilting the greens.
- Garnish salads with simple trims such as onion or green pepper rings, radish roses, olives, fruit, cherry tomatoes, edible flowers and nuts.

Mary Krekel, Illinois

CHICKEN VEGETABLE SALAD WITH DILL DRESSING

DRESSING
¼ cup lemon juice
¼ cup olive oil
1 teaspoon dried dill weed
¼ teaspoon salt
⅛ teaspoon black pepper

SALAD
4 cups GOURMET'S CHOICE California Blend
2 tablespoons oil
4 SCHWAN'S Unbreaded Chicken Breast Filets, cut in bite-size pieces
6 cups torn head lettuce
½ cup (cut into ½-inch pieces) green onions
½ cup sliced or quartered black olives, optional
3 ounces Bleu cheese, crumbled

In small bowl, combine all dressing ingredients; mix well, set aside. Thaw vegetables under running water; drain. Heat oil in large (12-inch) skillet over medium-high heat; sauté chicken for 4 to 5 minutes, or until lightly browned, stirring occasionally. In large bowl, combine vegetables, chicken, lettuce, onions, olives and Bleu cheese; toss gently. Pour dressing over salad; toss gently to coat. Cover and refrigerate until served. Refrigerate leftovers. 4 (1½-cup) servings.

Pauline Dornithorne, Oregon

CHINESE CHICKEN SALAD

SALAD

4 SCHWAN'S Unbreaded Chicken Breast Filets, cut into 2x½-inch strips
¼ cup cornstarch
½ cup oil, divided
1 medium head iceberg lettuce, thinly shredded (about 6 cups)
4 green onions, cut into 2-inch strips

DRESSING

¼ cup chunky peanut butter
¼ cup light or dark corn syrup
3 tablespoons white vinegar
2 tablespoons sesame seeds
1 teaspoon salt
⅛ teaspoon pepper

Place cornstarch in plastic bag; add chicken and shake to coat. Heat ¼ cup of the oil in large (12-inch) skillet over medium-high heat. Add 5 to 6 chicken pieces at a time to hot oil. Cook 3 to 4 minutes, or until golden brown, turning as needed. Drain on paper towels; cover and refrigerate.

In large bowl, combine lettuce and onions; cover and refrigerate. In small bowl, combine peanut butter, ¼ cup of the oil and corn syrup; mix well. Add vinegar, sesame seeds, salt and pepper; mix well. Cover; refrigerate. Just before serving, add chicken to lettuce mixture. Pour dressing over salad; toss gently. Refrigerate leftovers. 6 (1⅓-cup) servings.

Carol Ditkof, Michigan

ROTINI CHICKEN SALAD

8 cups GOURMET'S CHOICE Italian Pasta Blend
3 cups SCHWAN'S Diced Chicken Meat, thawed
¾ cup purchased coleslaw dressing

Thaw Italian pasta blend under running water; drain. In large bowl, combine Italian pasta blend, chicken and dressing; toss gently. Cover; refrigerate for 1 hour before serving. Refrigerate leftovers. 7 (1-cup) servings.

“*We've used Schwan's for many years – just because of the quality products that they offer.*”

Carol Ditkof

$5,000 Winner
Vicki Cohn, California

SCHWAN'S TURKEY-APRICOT SALAD

SALAD

3 LORI'S KITCHEN Unbreaded Turkey Breast Filets
2½ cups (8 oz.) uncooked spiral macaroni
1 teaspoon olive oil
4 fresh apricots, quartered, seeded OR 1 (16-oz.) can unpeeled apricot halves in juice, drained
1 small zucchini, julienned
1 yellow OR red bell pepper, thinly sliced
1 tablespoon chopped fresh basil OR 1 teaspoon dried basil leaves
1 teaspoon garlic powder
¼ teaspoon salt
⅛ teaspoon pepper
Lettuce, if desired

DRESSING

3 to 4 fresh apricots OR 1 (16-oz.) can unpeeled apricot halves in juice, drained
½ cup olive oil
¼ cup sugar
¼ cup vinegar
1 tablespoon chopped fresh basil OR 1 teaspoon dried basil leaves

Prepare turkey as directed on package. Slice into bite-size strips; set aside. Prepare macaroni as directed on package; drain, rinse with cold water. In large bowl, toss macaroni with 1 teaspoon oil. Add turkey and all remaining salad ingredients; toss gently.

In food processor with metal blade or in blender container, combine all dressing ingredients. Process with on-off pulse until smooth. Pour dressing over salad; toss gently to coat. If desired, serve on bed of lettuce. Refrigerate leftovers. 8 (1-cup) servings.

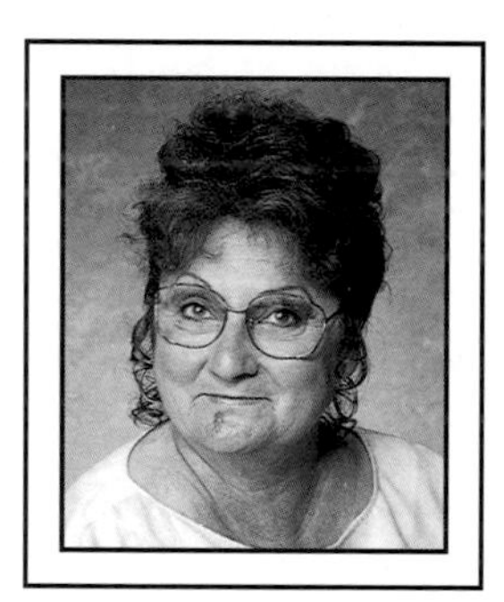

"My husband has been a fireman for 30 years and is gone every other day, so Schwan's makes it more convenient when it comes to preparing meals."

Vicki Cohn

Schwan's Turkey-Apricot Salad (top)
Chili-Chicken Salad (bottom) p.40

$1,000 Winner
Susan Grimm, Iowa

CHILI-CHICKEN SALAD

2 cups (12 oz.) SCHWAN'S Diced Chicken Meat, thawed
1 garlic clove, minced
2 tablespoons lemon juice
1½ teaspoons chili powder
½ teaspoon salt
1 large ripe avocado, peeled, pitted, cut into pieces
½ pint cherry tomatoes, cut in half (about 10)
¼ cup chopped red onions
½ cup dairy sour cream
Shredded lettuce

In large bowl, combine all ingredients *except* lettuce; toss gently. Serve over shredded lettuce. Refrigerate leftovers. 4 (1-cup) servings.

"A nice man came to my door one day and said Schwan's was having a special ice cream promotion, so I bought some ice cream and that started it."

Susan Grimm

Becky Carhoff, Iowa

CALICO SALAD

DRESSING
1 cup sugar
¾ cup cider vinegar
½ cup oil
1 tablespoon water
1 teaspoon salt
1 teaspoon pepper

SALAD
2 to 3 cups water
2 cups GOURMET'S CHOICE Cut Green Beans
2 cups GOURMET'S CHOICE Early Garden Blend
2 cups GOURMET'S CHOICE Cut Corn
1 cup chopped celery
1 cup chopped green bell pepper
½ cup chopped onions
½ cup chopped red bell pepper

In small saucepan over medium-high heat, combine all dressing ingredients; boil 1 minute. Allow to cool in saucepan.

Meanwhile, in large saucepan or Dutch oven bring water to boil. Place vegetables in steamer or colander over boiling water; cover. Steam 8 to 10 minutes or until crisply tender. Immediately place vegetables into ice water for 5 minutes; drain. Pour dressing over vegetables; toss gently to mix. Cover; refrigerate at least 4 hours. Refrigerate leftovers. 12 (½-cup) servings.

Karen Cook, Iowa

PRIMAVERA SALAD

SALAD
- 2 cups LORI'S KITCHEN Cheese Tortellini
- 1 (8-oz.) package GOURMET'S CHOICE Broccoli Spears
- 1 cup thinly sliced carrots
- ⅓ cup pitted ripe olives, sliced
- 1 medium red bell pepper, cut into thin strips
- Spinach leaves

DRESSING
- ⅓ cup mayonnaise
- ⅓ cup pesto sauce, if desired
- ¼ cup milk
- ¼ teaspoon pepper

Cook tortellini according to package directions; rinse with cold water, drain. Cook broccoli according to package directions; drain and cut into 1-inch pieces. In large bowl, combine tortellini, broccoli, carrots, olives and bell pepper; mix well.

In small bowl, combine dressing ingredients; mix well. Pour dressing over salad; toss until well combined. Cover; chill 4 to 24 hours. If desired, serve in spinach-lined bowl. Refrigerate leftovers. 4 (1¼-cup) servings.

Karen Kunz, Illinois

PASTA SHRIMP SALAD

SALAD
- 4 cups GOURMET'S CHOICE Italian Pasta Blend
- 4 cups SEAFARER'S CHOICE P & D Shrimp, cooked
- ½ cup chopped celery
- ½ cup chopped onions
- ½ cup chopped zucchini or cucumber
- 2 hard-cooked eggs, chopped
- ¼ teaspoon salt
- ⅛ teaspoon coarsely ground pepper

DRESSING
- ½ cup dairy sour cream
- ½ cup mayonnaise
- 1 tablespoon Worcestershire sauce
- 1 teaspoon lemon juice

In large bowl, combine all salad ingredients; toss gently. In small bowl, combine all dressing ingredients; mix well. Pour dressing over salad; toss gently to coat. Cover; refrigerate at least 2 hours to blend flavors. Refrigerate leftovers. 7 (1-cup) servings.

Schwan's TIP

Q: What is the quickest way to chill foods?

A: Place the bowl or saucepan of food in a container of ice water. Food can also be placed in the freezer for a short time. Twenty minutes in the freezer is equal to about an hour in the refrigerator.

Joan Enders, Washington

QUICK CURRIED CHICKEN TORTELLINI SALAD

SALAD

6 cups LORI'S KITCHEN Chicken Tortellini
2 cups chopped celery hearts
1½ cups halved red seedless grapes
1 cup sliced brown mushrooms
½ cup chopped green onions
Shredded lettuce

DRESSING

1 (8-oz.) container plain nonfat yogurt
½ cup reduced-calorie mayonnaise
1 tablespoon lemon juice
1 to 2 teaspoons curry powder
½ teaspoon salt

Prepare tortellini according to package directions; rinse with cold water and drain. In large bowl, combine tortellini, celery, grapes, mushrooms and onions; toss gently. In small bowl, combine all dressing ingredients; mix well. Pour over salad; toss gently. Cover; refrigerate 1 to 2 hours or until well chilled. Serve on shredded lettuce. Refrigerate leftovers. 9 (1-cup) servings.

Delores Sovereign, New York

SEAFOOD PASTA SALAD

1 (.07-oz.) packet dry Italian salad dressing
4 cups SEAFARER'S CHOICE P & D Shrimp, cooked
8 cups GOURMET'S CHOICE Italian Pasta Blend, thawed
1 (16-oz.) can pitted ripe olives, drained
8 ounces Cheddar cheese, cubed

Prepare dressing according to package directions; set aside. In large bowl, combine all remaining ingredients; mix well. Pour dressing over salad; toss gently to coat. Cover; refrigerate for 2 hours. Refrigerate leftovers. 9 (1-cup) servings.

Quick Curried Chicken Tortellini Salad (top)
Seafood Pasta Salad (bottom)

Marsha Broyles, Iowa

HONEY MIXED FRUIT SALAD

¼ cup honey
¼ cup lemon juice
¼ teaspoon ground cinnamon
1 bag GOURMET'S CHOICE Mixed Fruit, thawed, *un*drained

In small bowl, combine honey, lemon juice and cinnamon; mix well. In large bowl, place thawed fruit. Pour dressing over fruit; toss gently to coat. Refrigerate leftovers. 8 (½-cup) servings.

Corinne Bender, Illinois

MEDITERRANEAN TORTELLINI SALAD

3 cups LORI'S KITCHEN Cheese Tortellini
1 small red bell pepper, cut into thin strips
1 small green bell pepper, cut into thin strips
1 small yellow bell pepper, cut into thin strips
¼ cup pitted ripe olives, sliced
1 medium tomato, chopped
8 ounces feta cheese, crumbled
1 cup prepared Italian salad dressing

Cook tortellini according to package directions. Drain; rinse with cold water, set aside. In large bowl, combine all ingredients except bottled dressing; toss gently. Pour dressing over salad; toss gently to coat. Cover; refrigerate at least 2 hours. Toss gently just before serving. Refrigerate leftovers. 8 (1-cup) servings.

Linda Rasmussen, Idaho

ITALIAN VEGETABLE TOSS

8 cups GOURMET'S CHOICE Italian Pasta Blend
1 (6-oz.) can artichoke hearts, drained, rinsed and chopped
1 cup sliced ripe olives
½ cup chopped green onions
¾ cup prepared Italian salad dressing
1 medium avocado, peeled and sliced
1 medium tomato, seeded and chopped

Cook pasta blend according to package directions; drain. In large bowl, combine pasta blend, artichoke hearts, olives, green onions and Italian dressing; toss gently. Cover; refrigerate 2 to 3 hours to blend flavors. Just before serving, add avocado and tomato; toss gently. Refrigerate left-overs. 7 (1-cup) servings.

"I use SCHWAN'S products because when I get home it's nice to have something quick to fix from the freezer. We do enjoy the quality."

Linda Rasmussen

Jennie Forrister, Wyoming

SUMMER SURPRISE SALAD

4 cups GOURMET'S CHOICE Summer Garden Pasta Blend
1½ cups SCHWAN'S Diced Chicken
1 teaspoon dried oregano leaves
1 teaspoon parsley flakes
2 garlic cloves, minced
½ teaspoon salt
¼ teaspoon pepper
¼ cup salad dressing or mayonnaise

In large bowl, combine all ingredients *except* salad dressing; mix well. Add salad dressing; gently toss. Cover; refrigerate 1 hour. Just before serving, gently toss; serve immediately. Refrigerate leftovers. 4 (1-cup) servings.

"The Beginning, 1952."
A limited edition print commemorating the start of SCHWAN'S Home Food Service.

SIDE DISHES

Turn your entreés into a complete meal with these tasty and colorful accent dishes.

Tortellini Italiano p.48
Broccoli Pie p.49

Tortellini Italiano

Irene Bukowski, Illinois

TORTELLINI ITALIANO

1 (1½-lb.) bag LORI'S KITCHEN Cheese Tortellini
2 tablespoons olive oil
1 medium onion, sliced
1 garlic clove, minced
1 (14.5-oz.) can stewed tomatoes
1 (4-oz.) can sliced mushrooms, drained
1 tablespoon minced fresh parsley
1 teaspoon dried basil leaves
¼ teaspoon dried oregano leaves
2 tablespoons grated Parmesan cheese

Cook tortellini according to package directions; drain. Set aside and keep warm. Heat olive oil in medium saucepan; sauté onions and garlic until golden brown. Add tomatoes, mushrooms, parsley, basil and oregano. Cover; simmer 20 minutes, stirring occasionally.

Pour sauce over hot tortellini; sprinkle with Parmesan cheese. Refrigerate leftovers. 15 (½ cup) servings.

“*I've been a customer for years. Originally it was friends in the country who got me started.*”

Irene Bukowski

Cindy Aldrich, Michigan

BROCCOLI PIE

3 individual serving packets (6 cups) GOURMET'S CHOICE Broccoli Spears
1 cup chopped onions
1 9-inch unbaked pie crust
4 eggs, beaten
¼ teaspoon salt, if desired
8 slices SCHWAN'S American Processed Cheese
¼ cup grated Parmesan cheese

Heat oven to 350°F. Cook broccoli with onions according to package directions; drain, cool slightly and coarsely chop. In prepared pie crust, layer half of broccoli, half of eggs, half of salt and 4 slices of cheese; repeat layers. Sprinkle with Parmesan cheese. Bake at 350°F. for 40 to 50 minutes or until golden brown and eggs are set. Refrigerate leftovers. 8 servings.

Sally Judge, Oklahoma

GREEK TORTELLINI BAKE

1 (1½-lb.) bag LORI'S KITCHEN Cheese Tortellini
¼ cup butter, melted
¾ to 1 cup shredded mild colby cheese
4 eggs
½ cup milk
3 tablespoons grated Parmesan cheese
¼ teaspoon salt
⅛ teaspoon nutmeg
Cinnamon

Heat oven to 350°F. In 11x7-inch (2-quart) microwave-safe casserole, place tortellini. Cover with water. Microwave on HIGH for 3-5 minutes; drain. Pour butter over tortellini; stir. Sprinkle with colby cheese. In medium bowl, beat eggs and milk; add Parmesan cheese, salt and nutmeg. Pour egg mixture over tortellini; sprinkle with cinnamon.

Bake at 350°F., uncovered, for 30-40 minutes, or until egg mixture is set. Cut into squares to serve. Refrigerate leftovers. 8 servings.

NOTE: Microwave timings are for 700 to 800 watt microwave ovens. With an oven of different wattage outputs, timings may need slight adjustment.

Jewell Burton, Missouri

SCHWAN'S PEAS

1¾ cups GOURMET'S CHOICE Green Peas
2 teaspoons butter or margarine
½ cup mayonnaise*
1½ teaspoons lemon juice
⅛ teaspoon onion powder
⅛ teaspoon curry powder
⅛ teaspoon seasoned salt

Cook peas according to package directions; drain (reserve 2 teaspoons of liquid) and keep warm. Melt butter in medium saucepan over low heat. Add reserved liquid, mayonnaise, lemon juice, onion powder, curry powder and seasoned salt; mix well. Cook over low heat until warm; stir in peas. Refrigerate leftovers. 3 (½-cup) servings.

*TIP: ¼ cup mayonnaise and ¼ cup plain yogurt can be substituted for the mayonnaise.

Sally Judge, Oklahoma

DIJON GREEN BEAN BAKE

2½ cups GOURMET'S CHOICE Cut Green Beans
1 (10¾-oz.) cream of celery soup
2 teaspoons Dijon style mustard
½ teaspoon dried dill weed
⅛ to ¼ teaspoon white pepper or black pepper
½ cup soft bread crumbs

Heat oven to 350°F. In ungreased 8-inch square pan, combine all ingredients, *except* bread crumbs; mix well. Spread evenly in pan; top with bread crumbs. Bake, uncovered, at 350°F. for 45 minutes or until heated through. Refrigerate leftovers. 5 (½-cup) servings.

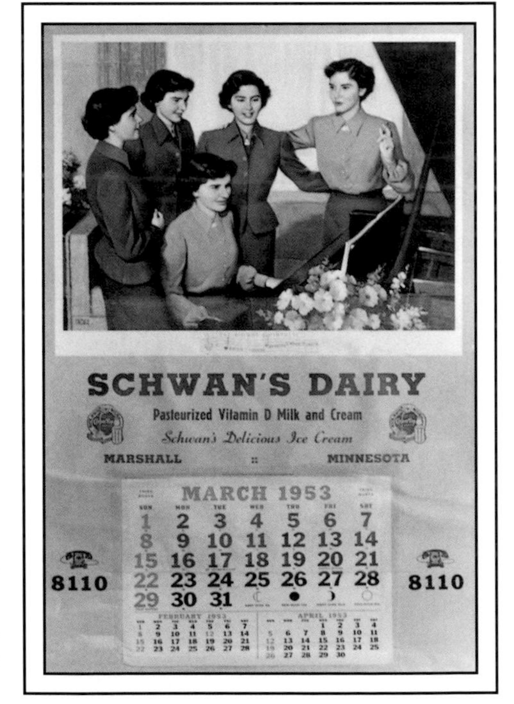

Back in 1953 Schwan's Dairy advertised their delicious ice cream with this calendar. Today Schwan's still produces America's "Most Cared For" Ice Cream®.

Toni Burkley, Pennsylvania

TANGY GREEN BEANS

½ cup finely minced green onions
2 tablespoons butter
4 cups (1 lb.) GOURMET'S CHOICE Cut Green Beans
1 to 2 tablespoons raspberry vinegar
½ teaspoon salt
⅛ teaspoon pepper

In large (12-inch) skillet over low heat, sauté green onions in butter 2 minutes or until tender; set aside. Cook green beans according to package directions until tender, but still crisp; drain. Add green beans, vinegar, salt and pepper to green onions; mix well. Refrigerate leftovers. 6 (½-cup) servings.

Margaret Taylor, Alabama

BABY CARROTS & CHEESE SAUCE

1 (2-lb.) pkg. GOURMET'S CHOICE Baby Carrots
10 slices SCHWAN'S American Processed Cheese
⅓ cup milk
1 teaspoon seasoned salt
¼ teaspoon black pepper
¼ teaspoon garlic powder
¼ teaspoon dried rosemary leaves

Cook carrots according to package directions; drain well. Keep warm. In small saucepan over low heat, combine milk and cheese. Cook and stir until cheese is melted. Add seasoned salt, pepper, garlic powder and rosemary; stir until well mixed. Spoon carrots into serving bowl; pour cheese sauce over carrots. Refrigerate leftovers. 11 (½-cup) servings.

Schwan's TIP

Q: How can I prevent cheese from becoming tough and rubbery when heating?

A: Use a low temperature and gently heat until cheese melts. Cheese will become tough and rubbery if overcooked or heated too quickly. Shred or cut cheese into small pieces to speed melting.

Margaret Howard, Texas

BUFFET PARTY PEAS

10 slices HAUGIN'S FARM BRAND Thick Sliced Bacon
1½ cups chopped onions
1 (2½-lb.) pkg. GOURMET'S CHOICE Green Peas
5 eggs, lightly beaten
Salt, if desired
Pepper, if desired

In large saucepan, cook peas according to package directions; drain. Return peas to saucepan and keep warm.

In large (12-inch) skillet, fry bacon until crisp; drain on paper toweling and reserve ¼ cup drippings. Sauté onions in 2 tablespoons of bacon drippings; place in saucepan with peas. In same skillet, scramble eggs in remaining 2 tablespoons bacon drippings. Add eggs to peas. Crumble bacon; add to peas and mix gently but thoroughly. Season to taste with salt and pepper. Refrigerate leftovers. 18 (½-cup) servings.

Lorraine Becraft, Nevada

PICKLED VEGETABLES

2 cups sugar
2 cups distilled white vinegar
1 cup boiling water
¼ cup pickling salt
1 to 2 garlic cloves, minced
4 cups GOURMET'S CHOICE California Blend, thawed

In large (8-cup) nonmetallic bowl, combine all ingredients except California Blend; mix well. Add California Blend; mix well. Cover; refrigerate 24 hours, stirring occasionally. Store covered in refrigerator. 8 (½-cup) servings.

Cindy Pinkerton, Texas

RAINBOW RICE DISH

½ cup sliced zucchini
⅓ cup chopped green onions
1½ cups GOURMET'S CHOICE IQF White Rice, cooked
1 cup GOURMET'S CHOICE Cut Corn, thawed
1 cup chopped tomatoes
2 tablespoons chopped fresh parsley
1 teaspoon dried oregano leaves
¾ teaspoon salt
⅛ teaspoon pepper
1 garlic clove, minced

Spray an electric skillet or wok with nonstick cooking spray; heat to350°F. Add zucchini and onions; cook and stir 2 minutes or until tender. Add rice, corn, tomatoes, parsley, oregano, salt, pepper and garlic; mix well. Cover; lower heat to 250°F. Simmer 10 minutes, stirring occasionally. Refrigerate leftovers. 5 (½-cup) servings.

TIPS: If mixture sticks during cooking, add 1 to 3 tablespoons water.

Mixture can be prepared in medium saucepan. Cook zucchini and onions over medium heat. Add remaining ingredients; cover and simmer over low heat for 10 minutes, stirring occasionally.

"I have had a great time experimenting with all of these great foods. Some of the recipes that I entered are from my first SCHWAN'S products used in 1988 when I lived in Dallas."

Cindy Pinkerton

Clockwise from Left:
Buffet Party Peas
Rainbow Rice Dish
Pickled Vegetables

Jean Schilling, Tennessee

TANGY CORN WITH GREEN PEPPERS

3 tablespoons butter or margarine
⅓ cup chopped green bell pepper
3 cups GOURMET'S CHOICE Cut Corn, thawed and drained
1 (8-oz) carton dairy sour cream
2 to 4 tablespoons salsa
¼ teaspoon salt, if desired

Melt butter in 1½-quart saucepan over low heat; add green pepper and sauté until tender. Add corn; sauté until tender, stirring frequently. Add sour cream, salsa and salt; stir over low heat until heated through. Refrigerate leftovers. 6 (½-cup) servings.

Suzy Unwin, Oklahoma

TORTELLINI CARBONARA

1 (1½ lb.) LORI'S KITCHEN Cheese Tortellini
1 garlic clove, minced
1½ teaspoons olive oil or reserved bacon grease
½ teaspoon vinegar
3 slices HAUGIN'S FARM BRAND Thick Sliced Bacon, cooked and crumbled
⅓ cup grated Parmesan cheese
¼ cup whipping cream or milk
1 tablespoon chopped fresh parsley
¼ teaspoon freshly ground pepper

Cook tortellini according to package directions.

In medium skillet (10-inch), sauté garlic in olive oil; stir in vinegar and tortellini. In small bowl, combine bacon, Parmesan cheese, cream, parsley and pepper; toss with tortellini. Refrigerate leftovers. 10 servings.

Theresa Rallo, Pennsylvania

CREAMY SPINACH & TORTELLINI

- **4 cups LORI'S KITCHEN Cheese Tortellini**
- **2 tablespoons olive oil**
- **½ cup chopped onion**
- **2 to 3 garlic cloves, minced**
- **4 to 5 cups GOURMET'S CHOICE Cut Leaf Spinach, thawed and drained**
- **1 cup seeded and chopped tomato**
- **1½ teaspoons dried basil leaves**
- **½ teaspoon salt**
- **¼ teaspoon pepper**
- **1½ cups milk**
- **2 tablespoons flour**
- **¼ cup grated Parmesan cheese**

Cook tortellini as directed on package; set aside.

Heat oil in large (12-inch) skillet over medium- high heat. Sauté onions and garlic until browned; add spinach, tomatoes, basil, salt and pepper. Cook 2 minutes, stirring occasionally. Whisk together milk and flour; add to spinach and cook 2 more minutes or until mixture boils and thickens. Add tortellini; mix well. Cook until hot. Stir in Parmesan cheese. Serve with additional Parmesan cheese, if desired. Refrigerate leftovers. 12 (½-cup) servings.

Pat Moracco, New York

ITALIAN STYLE SPINACH

- **⅓ to ½ cup olive oil**
- **4½ cups GOURMET'S CHOICE Cut Leaf Spinach**
- **½ teaspoon salt**
- **½ teaspoon pepper**
- **½ teaspoon garlic powder**
- **¼ cup Italian-flavored bread crumbs**
- **1 tablespoon grated Parmesan or Romano cheese**

Heat oil in medium (10-inch) skillet over high heat; add spinach, salt, pepper and garlic powder. Cook and stir 5 to 7 minutes, or until spinach is heated through. Add crumbs and cheese; mix well. Refrigerate leftovers. 5 (½-cup) servings.

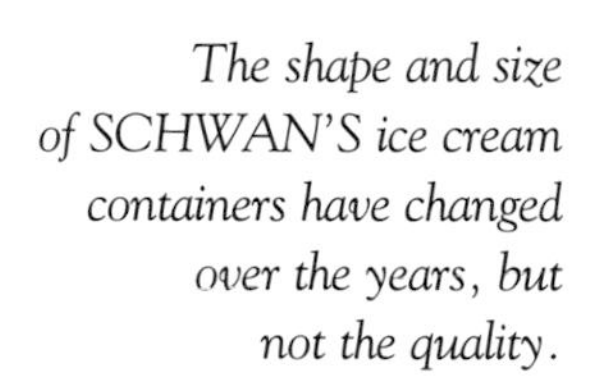

The shape and size of SCHWAN'S ice cream containers have changed over the years, but not the quality.

Becky Carhoff, Iowa

'INCA GOLD' SAUCE

24 slices (16-oz. pkg.) SCHWAN'S American Processed Cheese, cut up
1 (5-oz.) can evaporated milk
2 teaspoons Worcestershire sauce
1½ teaspoons dry mustard
1½ teaspoons dried minced onions
⅛ teaspoon pepper
1 cup dairy sour cream

In top of double boiler over simmering water, combine cut-up cheese, evaporated milk, Worcestershire sauce, mustard, onions and pepper. Heat thoroughly (*do not allow to boil*), stirring until smooth. Add sour cream; mix well. Serve immediately or cover and store in refrigerator. 3 cups.

TIP: To make in microwave oven, in microwave-safe casserole, place cheese, evaporated milk, Worcestershire sauce, dry mustard, onion and pepper. Microwave on HIGH for 5 minutes, stirring 3 times, until cheese is melted and mixture is smooth. Stir in sour cream; microwave on HIGH for 1½ to 2 minutes, stirring twice, until heated.

NOTE: Microwave timings are for 700 to 800 watt microwave ovens. With an oven of different wattage output, timings may need slight adjustment.

SERVING SUGGESTIONS

VEGETABLE SAUCE: Cook a package of GOURMET'S CHOICE vegetables and spoon sauce over.

BAKED POTATO TOPPING: Put a spoonful on top of a baked potato and sprinkle with cooked and crumbled HAUGIN'S FARM BRAND Thick Sliced Bacon.

HOT DIP: Serve hot with fresh crisp vegetables.

SANDWICH SPREAD: Refrigerate and use as spread with HAUGIN'S FARM Ham. Can add pimiento before spreading on bread.

MACARONI AND CHEESE: Cook pasta as directed; drain and stir in desired amount of sauce.

WELSH RAREBIT: Serve over toasted SCHWAN'S Honey Wheat Bread. Garnish with sweet pickles and sliced tomatoes.

NACHOS: Combine 1 cup sauce and ½ cup sliced jalapeño peppers or ½ cup salsa; serve with corn chips.

"*I have such fond memories as a child when my mother would serve SCHWAN'S ice cream treats with little green Christmas trees in the middle to us at each Christmas Eve supper. Now I have my own traditions to pass on to my daughters.*"

Becky Carhoff

'Inca Gold' Sauce with Schwan's Broccoli Spears

Carol Jones, Texas

DELICIOUS POLISH DUMPLINGS

6 cups water
12 LORI'S KITCHEN Pierogies
2 tablespoons butter
½ cup chopped onions
½ cup dairy sour cream
3 tablespoons sugar

In 2-quart saucepan, boil water. Add pierogies; return to a boil. Boil for 5 minutes; drain. Meanwhile, melt butter over low heat in large (12-inch) skillet; sauté onions. Add pierogies. Over medium heat, sauté pierogies on one side for 5 to 8 minutes; turn and sauté other side for about 4 minutes, or until both sides are lightly browned. Serve with sour cream and sugar. Refrigerate leftovers. 6 servings.

Schwan's TIP

Q: Can white pepper be used in place of black pepper?

A: Since it's less obvious, use white pepper in any recipe where you want to avoid seeing black specks.

Sandra Carney, Maryland

BEST RICE CASSEROLE

1 (1½ lb.) bag GOURMET'S CHOICE IQF White Rice, cooked
1 (8-oz.) can or 2 (4-oz.) cans sliced mushrooms, drained
¼ cup butter or margarine
¼ cup chopped onions
2 tablespoons finely chopped celery
1 garlic clove, minced
1 tablespoon dried parsley
1 teaspoon seasoned salt
¼ cup butter or margarine
3 tablespoons flour
1 cup milk
1 (8-oz.) pkg. cream cheese, softened

Heat oven to 350°F. In large bowl, combine rice and mushrooms; set aside. Melt ¼ cup butter in medium (10-inch) skillet. Add onions, celery, garlic, parsley and seasoned salt; sauté until onions are tender. Combine with rice mixture.

In same skillet, melt ¼ cup butter over low heat; stir in flour until well blended. Add milk; cook and stir until thickened and bubbly. Add cream cheese; cook and stir just until melted and mixture is smooth. Spoon half of rice mixture into ungreased 11x7-inch pan; cover with half of cream cheese mixture. Repeat. Bake, uncovered, at 350°F. for 30 to 40 minutes or until heated through. Refrigerate leftovers. 14 (½-cup) servings.

Dolores Mollica, Florida

SPINACH CHEESE SURPRISE

5 eggs
1 teaspoon garlic powder
½ to 1 teaspoon salt
½ teaspoon ground pepper
4½ cups GOURMET'S CHOICE Cut Leaf Spinach, thawed, well drained, chopped
2 cups shredded Cheddar cheese
½ cup milk
1 tablespoon Italian-flavored bread crumbs

Heat oven to 350°F. Spray an 8-inch square baking dish with nonstick cooking spray; set aside. In medium bowl, beat together eggs, garlic powder, salt and pepper. Add spinach, cheese and milk; mix well and spoon into prepared pan. Sprinkle bread crumbs on top. Bake at 350°F. for 40 to 50 minutes or until golden brown and eggs are set. Refrigerate leftovers. 6 servings.

Suzette Modispaugh, West Virginia

QUIK TATER® PACKETS

1 cup GOURMET'S CHOICE QUIK TATERS
¼ medium onion, sliced
¼ medium green bell pepper, chopped
Salt to taste
Pepper to taste
1 teaspoon margarine

Heat oven to 350°F. In piece of aluminum foil (12x15-inch), place all ingredients; fold securely. Bake at 350°F. for 50 to 60 minutes, or until vegetables are tender. 1 serving.

TIP: Foil packets may be cooked on grill or campfire.

SCHWAN'S ice cream and Summer… a tradition that started back in the 50's, as this newspaper ad illustrates.

MAIN DISHES

Whether you're feeding a crowd or sharing a small family supper, these entrées offer a wide range of choices – spice it up with Breakfast Burritos or speed it up with Fast Fiesta Chicken!

Chicken Sweet & Sour Stir-Fry p.62

Chicken Sweet & Sour Stir-Fry

$1,000 Winner
Sonja King, Montana

CHICKEN SWEET & SOUR STIR-FRY

"I make sure I have things in the freezer from Schwan's. It's nice to have something easy to pop in the oven."

Sonja King

2 cups SCHWAN'S Popcorn Chicken Strips
1 tablespoon butter
5½ cups GOURMET'S CHOICE Stir-Fry Vegetables
½ cup prepared sweet and sour sauce

Heat oven to 350°F. Place chicken in 9-inch square pan. Bake at 350°F. for 15 to 20 minutes or until hot. About 5 minutes before chicken is done, melt butter in large (12-inch) skillet over medium-high heat. Add vegetables and stir-fry until hot, about 5 minutes. Add sweet and sour sauce to chicken; stir gently. Place vegetables on serving plate and top with chicken. Refrigerate leftovers. 2 servings.

Christina Hudson, Ohio

ONE-PAN STIR-FRY

2 tablespoons oil, divided
4 cups SCHWAN'S Diced Chicken Meat
1 garlic clove, minced
1½ cups GOURMET'S CHOICE Stir-Fry Vegetables
2 ounces angel hair pasta, broken in half
1 (14½-oz.) can (1⅔ cups) chicken broth
2 tablespoons low-sodium soy sauce
1 tablespoon cornstarch
2 tablespoons cooking sherry or water

In wok or large (12-inch) skillet, heat 1 tablespoon oil over high heat. Add chicken; stir constantly until heated. Remove chicken. Add remaining 1 tablespoon oil to wok. Add garlic and vegetables; sauté until heated.
Add angel hair pasta, chicken and chicken broth. Bring to a boil; reduce heat, cover and simmer 4 to 5 minutes. Remove cover and cook for 2 minutes, stirring frequently.

In small bowl, combine soy sauce, cornstarch and sherry. Add to wok; cook, stirring constantly, until thickened. Serve immediately. Refrigerate leftovers. 4 servings.

Rod Repka, Illinois

PLUM CHICKEN STIR-FRY

4 cups SCHWAN'S Diced Chicken Meat
11 cups GOURMET'S CHOICE Stir-Fry Vegetables
2 tablespoons oriental plum sauce
1 tablespoon soy sauce or to taste
1 cup dry roasted peanuts
1 cup chopped green onion tops
4 to 6 cups cooked GOURMET'S CHOICE IQF White Rice

Thaw chicken for 2 minutes in microwave.

Spray wok with nonstick cooking spray. Over high heat, stir-fry chicken for 2 minutes. Remove chicken. Add vegetables to wok and stir-fry for 2 to 3 minutes or until vegetables are hot. Add chicken, plum sauce and soy sauce to vegetables; cook 2 minutes. Stir in peanuts and green onion tops. Serve over cooked rice with LORI'S KITCHEN Chicken Egg Rolls. Refrigerate leftovers. 6 to 8 servings.

Diane Davidson, Texas

CHICKEN FAJITA STIR-FRY

- 2 teaspoons oil
- 3 garlic cloves, minced
- 1½ teaspoons minced fresh gingerroot (about a 1-inch piece)
- 1 or 2 jalapeño peppers, seeded and chopped
- 5 cups SCHWAN'S Chicken Breast Meat for Fajitas
- 11 cups GOURMET'S CHOICE Stir-Fry Vegetables
- 3 tablespoons low-sodium soy sauce
- 5 green onions, diagonally sliced in ½-inch pieces
- 4 to 5 cups cooked GOURMET'S CHOICE IQF White Rice
- Low-sodium soy sauce

Heat oil in large wok over high heat. Add garlic, ginger and jalapeño pepper; stir-fry 30 seconds. Add chicken and stir-fry 2 minutes. Add vegetables and continue stir-frying 5 minutes or until vegetables are tender. Add soy sauce and green onions; lower heat and stir-fry 5 to 7 minutes.

Serve immediately over rice with additional soy sauce. Refrigerate leftovers. 6 servings.

Pam Bunn, Michigan

CHICKEN FAJITA ORIENTAL

- 5 cups (14-oz. bag) SCHWAN'S Chicken Breast Meat for Fajitas
- 1½ cups chicken broth
- 12 to 16 SEAFARER'S CHOICE P & D Shrimp, thawed
- 1 cup GOURMET'S CHOICE Stir-Fry Vegetables
- 2 tablespoons cornstarch
- ¼ cup cold water
- 4 cups cooked GOURMET'S CHOICE IQF White Rice
- ½ cup chow mein noodles, if desired

In large (12-inch) skillet over medium heat, cook chicken in chicken broth until thawed, about 5 minutes. Add shrimp and vegetables; continue cooking until hot, about 3 to 5 minutes, stirring occasionally. In small bowl, mix cornstarch and water; add to chicken mixture and cook until thickened, about 1 minute.

Serve immediately over rice. Sprinkle with chow mein noodles, if desired. Refrigerate leftovers. 6 to 8 servings.

"*I buy the majority of my meat and vegetables from Schwan's.*"

Pam Bunn

Carol Craig, Missouri

CHICKEN ENCHILADAS

- 1 (16-oz.) tub LORI'S KITCHEN Wisconsin Cheese Deli Soup
- 1½ cups GOURMET'S CHOICE Green Peas
- 2 cups chopped fresh tomato or 1 (14½-oz.) can chopped tomatoes
- 1 (16-oz.) can refried beans
- ½ cup chopped onions
- ¼ cup diced green bell pepper
- 1 to 2 tablespoons diced jalapeño pepper
- 1 teaspoon chili powder
- 1 teaspoon garlic powder
- ½ to 1 teaspoon salt, if desired
- Dash hot pepper sauce, if desired
- 1 (8-oz.) container dairy sour cream
- 5 cups (14 ounces) SCHWAN'S Chicken Breast Meat for Fajitas or 4 cups (12 ounces) SCHWAN'S Diced Chicken Meat
- 2 tablespoons oil
- 15 to 18 flour tortillas, heated
- 2 cups shredded Cheddar cheese
- Shredded lettuce
- Dairy sour cream

In large saucepan, combine soup, peas, tomatoes, refried beans, onions, bell peppers, jalapeño peppers, chili powder, garlic powder, salt and hot pepper sauce. Cook over medium heat about 7 to 10 minutes, or until hot, stirring frequently. Stir in sour cream; remove from heat and set aside.

Heat oven to 350°F. In medium (10-inch) skillet, sauté chicken in oil until hot, about 4 minutes. Add chicken to soup mixture; cool slightly. Spread ½ cup of the chicken mixture in 13x9-inch pan. Spread ¼ cup chicken mixture on each heated tortilla, roll up tightly and place on chicken mixture in pan. Spoon remaining chicken mixture over top; sprinkle with cheese. Bake at 350°F. for 20 to 30 minutes. Garnish with lettuce and sour cream. Refrigerate leftovers. 6 to 8 servings.

VARIATION

LOWFAT: Substitute no-fat sour cream, no-fat refried beans and no-fat Cheddar cheese for the regular sour cream, refried beans and Cheddar cheese.

Schwan's TIP

Create a casual party around this south-of-the-border entree. Serve along with refried beans, Spanish rice, chips and salsa. Decorate with colorful blankets, dolls and sombreros.

Sally Hunt, New York

MARCO POLO CASSEROLE

6 cups warm mashed potatoes
8 ounces deli-sliced boiled ham
6 to 8 GOURMET'S CHOICE Broccoli Spears, cooked and drained*
2 cups SCHWAN'S Diced Chicken Meat, thawed
1 (16-oz.) tub LORI'S KITCHEN Wisconsin Cheese Deli Soup, thawed

Heat oven to 350°F. Lightly spray a 13x9-inch pan with nonstick cooking spray. In prepared pan, layer potatoes, ham, broccoli spears and chicken. Spoon soup over chicken.

Bake at 350°F. for 40 to 50 minutes. Let stand 5 to 10 minutes before serving. Refrigerate leftovers. 6 to 8 servings.

*TIP: For ease in serving, cut broccoli into single spears.

Betty Hausauer, North Dakota

FAST FIESTA CHICKEN

1 tablespoon oil
2 cups SCHWAN'S Diced Chicken Meat
5 cups GOURMET'S CHOICE Italian Pasta Blend
¾ cup salsa
1 tablespoon chopped fresh cilantro, if desired

Heat oil in large (12-inch) skillet; cook chicken 2 to 3 minutes, or until hot. Add Italian Pasta Blend and salsa. Cover; simmer over medium heat 8 to 10 minutes or until vegetables are crisply tender, stirring occasionally. Stir in cilantro, if desired. Refrigerate leftovers. 4 servings.

Fast Fiesta Chicken

Larry Larason, Arizona

RAMEN SUPREME

- 1 (3-oz.) package chicken flavor ramen noodles OR ramen oriental noodle soup
- 1½ cups water
- ¾ to 1 cup GOURMET'S CHOICE California Blend
- ½ to ¾ cup diced SCHWAN'S Chicken Breast Meat for Fajitas
- 2 tablespoons chopped green onions, if desired
- Dash pepper OR hot pepper sauce

Crumble ramen noodles; set aside.

In medium saucepan over high heat, combine water, vegetables, chicken and onions; bring to a boil. Reduce heat; stir in noodles. Cool and stir until noodles are slightly soft. Stir in ramen flavor packet, pepper or hot sauce. Cook and stir 1 to 2 minutes or until noodles are done. Refrigerate leftovers. 1 serving.

Carolyn Cutlip-Griffith, Pennsylvania

DOUBLE POTATO-CHICKEN DELITE

- 1 (10¾-oz.) can cream of chicken soup
- ¾ cup dairy sour cream or plain yogurt
- ¼ cup milk or water
- 1 cup SCHWAN'S Diced Chicken Meat, thawed
- 2 to 3 cups shredded Cheddar cheese, divided
- 8 GOURMET'S CHOICE Shredded Hashbrowns
- 1 (2.8-oz.) can French-fried onions, crushed
- 1 cup coarsely crushed sour cream and onion potato chips
- 25 pieces SCHWAN'S Popcorn Chicken Strips

Heat oven to 350°F. In medium bowl, combine soup, sour cream, milk, diced chicken and ½ of the cheese; spread ¾ cup in bottom of greased 12x8-inch (2-quart) baking pan. Arrange hashbrowns on top and press down gently. Spread with remaining soup mixture, crushed onions, remaining cheese and crushed potato chips.

Bake at 350°F. for 50 minutes; remove from oven and top with popcorn chicken. Return to oven for 10 to 15 minutes. Let stand for 5 to 10 minutes before cutting into squares to serve. Refrigerate leftovers.
8 to 10 servings.

Lorraine Kay, Utah

CHICKEN VEGETABLE PASTA PRIMAVERA

8 cups water
1 tablespoon oil
6 ounces linguine, broken in half
1 cup boiling water
1 tablespoon chicken bouillon granules
5 cups SCHWAN'S Chicken Breast Meat for Fajitas
2½ cups GOURMET'S CHOICE California Blend
½ cup GOURMET'S CHOICE Green Peas
1½ teaspoons dried basil leaves
½ teaspoon garlic salt
¼ teaspoon pepper
2 tablespoons butter or margarine
¼ cup grated Parmesan cheese

Bring 8 cups water and oil to boil in large saucepan; add linguine. Cook for 8 to 10 minutes; drain.

In small bowl, mix 1 cup boiling water and chicken bouillon granules; set aside. In 3-quart microwave-safe casserole, place linguine, chicken, vegetables, basil, garlic salt and pepper; dot with butter. Add chicken broth; mix well. Microwave on HIGH, uncovered, for 15 to 20 minutes, or until hot, stirring after 7 minutes. Stir in Parmesan cheese. Refrigerate leftovers.
6 servings.

NOTE: Microwave timings are for 700 to 800 watt microwave ovens. With an oven of different wattage output, timings may need slight adjustment.

Darlene Mann, Texas

SPICY CHICKEN AND CABBAGE

2 teaspoons chicken bouillon granules
½ cup water
4 cups (12-oz. bag) SCHWAN'S Diced Chicken Meat
1 (1-lb.) pkg. ready-cut cole slaw mix
½ teaspoon coarsely ground black pepper
1 tablespoon cornstarch
¼ cup cold water
1½ to 3 teaspoons hot pepper sauce
3½ cups (6-oz. pkg.) chow mein noodles

In wok, over medium-high heat, dissolve chicken bouillon in ½ cup water. Add chicken; stir-fry until hot. Add cole slaw mix and pepper. If liquid has evaporated, add ¼ cup water. Stir-fry 1 minute, cover and steam 2 minutes.

Meanwhile, in small bowl, dissolve cornstarch in ¼ cup water. Add hot pepper sauce; pour over chicken. Stir-fry 1 minute or until thickened. Serve over chow mein noodles. Refrigerate leftovers.
4 to 6 servings.

“My sister had SCHWAN'S Home Delivery at her house and that's what got me started. It's so convenient. I've been a customer for years.”

Darlene Mann

Sandie Parker, Michigan

RASPBERRY BARBECUE CHICKEN

1 cup frozen unsweetened red raspberries, thawed, reserve ¼ cup juice
1 cup smoky barbecue sauce
¾ cup raspberry preserves or jelly
2 tablespoons butter or margarine
5 cups (14-oz. bag) SCHWAN'S Chicken Breast Meat for Fajitas, thawed

In small saucepan over low heat, combine raspberry juice, barbecue sauce and preserves or jelly; heat 3 to 4 minutes. Keep warm. Melt butter in medium (10-inch) skillet over medium-high heat. Add chicken and stir-fry for 5 minutes. Add sauce to chicken; stir to coat. Continue cooking for 3 minutes. Serve topped with thawed raspberries. Refrigerate leftovers. 4 to 6 servings.

Stephanie Fightmaster, Kentucky

YAH-HOO CHICKEN

5 cups SCHWAN'S Chicken Breast Meat for Fajitas
1 cup barbecue sauce
½ cup shredded Monterey Jack cheese
½ cup shredded colby cheese
4 cups cooked GOURMET'S CHOICE IQF White Rice, if desired
1 cup (1 large) chopped tomato
¼ cup chopped green onions

Heat oven to 375°F. In 9-inch square pan, place frozen chicken. Pour barbecue sauce over chicken and stir to coat; sprinkle with cheeses. Bake at 375°F. for 20 to 25 minutes or until heated and cheese is melted. Serve alone or over rice, topped with tomato and green onions. Refrigerate leftovers.
4 to 5 servings.

Yah-Hoo Chicken

Joanne Johnson, South Dakota

CHICKEN PITA FILLING

¼ cup mayonnaise
¼ cup dairy sour cream
2 teaspoons SCHWAN'S Orange Juice Concentrate, thawed, undiluted
¼ teaspoon salt
¼ teaspoon ground ginger
2 cups SCHWAN'S Diced Chicken Meat, thawed
1 cup halved green grapes
½ cup thinly sliced celery
1 cup alfalfa sprouts
6 to 8 (6½-inch) pitas

In small bowl, combine mayonnaise, sour cream, orange juice concentrate, salt and ginger; set aside. In medium bowl, combine chicken, grapes and celery; stir in mayonnaise mixture, mixing well. Using a fork, gently stir in alfalfa sprouts. Fill pitas. Refrigerate leftovers. 6 to 8 servings.

Chicken Pita Filling

Elaine Sisino, New York

CHICKEN BREASTS ALIDA

1½ cups seasoned fine dry bread crumbs
¼ cup grated Parmesan cheese
3 tablespoons sesame seed
8 SCHWAN'S Unbreaded Chicken Breast Filets, thawed
½ cup butter, melted

SAUCE

1 (10-oz.) jar red OR black currant jelly
⅔ cup SCHWAN'S Orange Juice Concentrate
1 tablespoon sherry wine
1 teaspoon dry mustard

Heat oven to 375°F. In small bowl, combine bread crumbs, cheese and sesame seed; place on waxed paper. Dip chicken in butter and then in crumbs. Place in 13x9-inch pan; drizzle with remaining butter. Bake, uncovered, at 375°F. for 30 minutes, or until chicken is no longer pink inside.

Meanwhile, in a small saucepan, combine jelly, orange juice concentrate, wine and mustard. Simmer over low heat, stirring to melt jelly, about 5 minutes; keep warm. Pour sauce over chicken to serve. Refrigerate leftovers. 8 servings.

Agnes Jennings, North Dakota

CHICKEN SALTIMBOCA

6 SCHWAN'S Unbreaded Chicken Breast Filets, thawed
¼ teaspoon salt, if desired
6 thin slices HAUGIN'S FARM BRAND Ham
⅔ cup (1 medium) chopped tomato
6 slices SCHWAN'S American Processed Cheese or Swiss cheese
½ teaspoon dried sage leaves
⅓ cup fine dry bread crumbs
2 tablespoons grated Parmesan cheese
2 tablespoons minced fresh parsley
4 tablespoons butter, melted

Heat oven to 350°F. Grease a 12x8-inch (2-quart) baking dish. Flatten chicken breasts by placing 1 breast at a time between 2 pieces of waxed paper; working from center, gently pound with rolling pin or meat mallet until about ¼-inch thick. Sprinkle flattened chicken breast with salt, if desired. Top with a slice of ham, chopped tomato, slice of cheese and sage; roll up and secure with toothpicks. In flat dish, combine crumbs, Parmesan cheese and parsley; dip chicken rolls in melted butter, then into crumb mixture. Place in prepared baking dish.

Bake, uncovered, at 350°F. for 30 to 40 minutes or until chicken is no longer pink inside. Refrigerate leftovers. 6 servings.

Sharon Bourbeau, Oklahoma

CASHEW CHICKEN

4 SCHWAN'S Unbreaded Chicken Breast Filets, thawed
¼ cup soy sauce
2 tablespoons cornstarch
½ teaspoon sugar
½ teaspoon salt, if desired
¼ cup oil, divided
¾ cup (4 oz.) cashews
2 cups GOURMET'S CHOICE Sugar Snap Peas, thawed
3 cups (8 oz.) sliced fresh mushrooms
4 green onions, cut into 1-inch pieces
1 (8-oz.) can sliced bamboo shoots, drained
1 cup chicken broth
Cooked GOURMET'S CHOICE IQF White Rice

Cut thawed chicken into 1-inch squares; set aside. In small bowl, combine soy sauce, cornstarch, sugar and salt; mix thoroughly and set aside. Heat 1 tablespoon oil in electric skillet set at 350°F. Add cashews; cook 1 minute, stirring constantly. Remove cashews from skillet. Add 3 tablespoons oil to skillet; cook chicken 2 minutes or until chicken is no longer pink. Add snap peas, mushrooms, onions and broth; cover and simmer 2 minutes. Add bamboo shoots and soy sauce mixture; cook, stirring constantly, until thickened. Simmer 1 minute and sprinkle with nuts. Serve over cooked rice. Refrigerate leftovers. 4 to 6 servings.

Denise Williams, Arkansas

CHICKEN PARMIGIANA

- 1 egg, beaten
- 1 teaspoon salt
- ¼ teaspoon pepper
- 6 to 8 SCHWAN'S Unbreaded Chicken Breast Filets
- 1 cup fine dry bread crumbs
- ½ cup butter
- 1 small (¾ lb.) eggplant, cut into ¾-inch slices
- 1 (15-oz.) can pizza sauce
- 6 slices mozzarella cheese
- 2 tablespoons grated Parmesan cheese

In shallow pan, combine egg, salt and pepper; dip chicken into egg mixture and then into crumbs.

Melt butter in large (12-inch) skillet; sauté chicken about 5 minutes or until lightly browned. In crockpot, place eggplant slices; top with chicken and pan drippings. Cover with sauce. Cover and cook on LOW for 6 to 8 hours. Add mozzarella cheese and Parmesan cheese. Cover; let stand 10 to 15 minutes to melt the cheeses. Refrigerate leftovers. 6 to 8 servings.

TIP: Place eggplant on bottom of crockpot or it will not cook completely.

" *We use SCHWAN'S vegetables, meats, pizzas – and the novelties for after-school snacks. SCHWAN'S ice cream is the only kind we have in our freezer.* **"**

Denise Williams

Julie Brown, North Carolina

ITALIAN CHICKEN

- 6 SCHWAN'S Unbreaded Chicken Breast Filets, thawed
- ½ cup chopped onions
- 2 teaspoons minced fresh garlic
- 1 teaspoon dried basil leaves
- ½ teaspoon dried oregano leaves
- ¼ to ½ teaspoon salt
- ¼ to ½ teaspoon pepper
- 2 (14½-oz.) cans diced tomatoes
- 1 cup shredded mozzarella cheese
- ¼ cup grated Parmesan cheese
- Cooked GOURMET'S CHOICE IQF White Rice

Heat oven to 325°F. Spray 13x9-inch baking pan with nonstick cooking spray. Layer ingredients in prepared pan in order given. Bake, uncovered, at 325°F. for 30 to 45 minutes or until chicken is no longer pink inside. Serve over rice. Refrigerate leftovers. 6 servings.

Schwan's TIP

Q: Are ingredients listed in any particular order on packaged food products?

A: The predominant ingredient is listed first with the remaining ingredients listed in descending order according to their weight in the package.

Tina Burrett, Pennsylvania

SCHWAN'S STUFFED CHICKEN

8 SCHWAN'S Unbreaded Chicken Breast Filets
1 tub LORI'S KITCHEN Cream of Broccoli Soup
1 tub LORI'S KITCHEN Wisconsin Cheese Deli Soup
6 to 8 slices SCHWAN'S American Processed Cheese
1 (8-oz.) pkg. chicken flavor one-step stuffing mix
½ cup butter, melted

Heat oven to 375°F. Place chicken breasts in 13x9-inch pan; top with broccoli soup, cheese soup and American cheese. Sprinkle with stuffing mix; drizzle with butter.

Bake, uncovered, at 375°F. for 50 minutes. Remove cover; bake 12 minutes or until stuffing is browned and chicken is no longer pink inside. Refrigerate leftovers. 8 servings.

Eunice Flourney, Oklahoma

CHICKEN ROLL-UPS

4 SCHWAN'S Unbreaded Chicken Breast Filets, thawed
4 thin slices HAUGIN'S FARM BRAND Ham
4 slices SCHWAN'S American Processed Cheese
2 tablespoons oil
1 (16-oz.) tub LORI'S KITCHEN Cream of Broccoli Soup
⅓ cup milk
¼ cup sliced green onions
⅛ teaspoon dried thyme leaves, crushed
2 tablespoons chopped fresh parsley, if desired

Flatten chicken breasts by placing 1 breast at a time between 2 pieces of waxed paper; working from center, gently pound chicken with rolling pin or meat mallet until about ¼-inch thick. Place a slice of ham and a slice of cheese on each flattened chicken breast. Roll up from narrow end and secure with toothpicks. In medium (10-inch) skillet, heat oil; cook chicken for 10 minutes, turning to evenly brown all sides. Spoon off drippings; add remaining ingredients *except* parsley. Heat to boiling; cover, reduce heat to low and simmer 10 minutes or until chicken is no longer pink. Sprinkle with parsley, if desired. Refrigerate leftovers. 4 servings.

Chicken Roll-Ups

Susan Bailey, Illinois

MICROWAVE SWEET TANGY CHICKEN

4 SCHWAN'S Unbreaded Chicken Breast Filets, thawed
½ cup peach preserves
¼ cup Italian dressing
2 tablespoons onion soup mix

In 8-inch square microwave-safe dish, place chicken breasts with edges of chicken touching sides of dish. In small bowl, stir together preserves, dressing and soup mix; pour over chicken. Cover with waxed paper; microwave on HIGH for 10 minutes. Rotate dish and baste chicken with sauce; cover and microwave 1 to 1½ additional minutes or until chicken is no longer pink inside. Let stand 5 minutes before serving. Refrigerate leftovers. 4 servings.

TIP: Serve with GOURMET'S CHOICE IQF White Rice or Broccoli Spears.

NOTE: Microwave timings are for 700 to 800 watt microwave ovens. With an oven of different wattage output, timings may need slight adjustment.

Karen Memmer, Indiana

LEMON CHICKEN & VEGETABLES

2 tablespoons olive oil or oil
4 small red potatoes, quartered
1 small onion, cut into 8 wedges
1 small (about ¼ lb.) yellow squash, cut into ½-inch slices
5½ cups GOURMET'S CHOICE California Blend
4 SCHWAN'S Unbreaded Chicken Breast Filets
¼ teaspoon salt
2 tablespoons SCHWAN'S Lemonade Concentrate,* thawed
¾ teaspoon salt
½ teaspoon dried thyme leaves
¼ teaspoon pepper
2 tablespoons hot water

Heat oven to 425°F. Place oil in 13x9-inch pan; heat in oven. In medium bowl, combine potatoes, onion, squash and California Blend. Place chicken breasts in hot oil and sprinkle with ¼ teaspoon salt. Bake at 425°F. for 5 minutes if thawed or 10 minutes if frozen. Remove from oven; turn chicken over. Add vegetables to pan; sprinkle with lemonade concentrate, ¾ teaspoon salt, thyme and pepper. Bake at 425°F. for 30 to 35 minutes, stirring once, or until vegetables are tender and chicken is no longer pink inside.

Arrange chicken and vegetables on plates. Add hot water to pan drippings; stir to loosen brown bits and pour over chicken. Refrigerate leftovers. 4 servings.

*TIP: Shake lemonade concentrate carton before measuring.

Lori Kozar, Virginia

CHICKEN CHIMAYO

¾ cup dry white wine
½ cup catsup
¼ cup minced onions
3½ tablespoons Worcestershire sauce
3 tablespoons white vinegar
¼ cup flour
1½ teaspoons salt
1 teaspoon paprika
5 SCHWAN'S Unbreaded Chicken Breast Filets
¼ cup vegetable oil
1 (4-oz.) can diced green chilies, undrained
½ to ¾ cup shredded Cheddar cheese
4 cups cooked GOURMET'S CHOICE IQF White Rice
Avocado slices, if desired
GOURMET'S CHOICE Cut Corn

In small bowl, combine wine, catsup, onions, Worcestershire sauce and vinegar; mix well and set aside. In plastic bag, combine flour, salt and paprika; shake chicken in mixture to coat. Heat oil in large (12-inch) skillet over medium-high heat. Brown chicken in oil; add wine mixture. Reduce heat; cover and simmer 10 minutes. Add ½ of the chilies with liquid; simmer, covered, 40 to 45 minutes.

Meanwhile, add remaining ½ of the chilies and cheese to hot rice. Place rice mixture on warm platter. Top with chicken breasts and spoon sauce over rice. Garnish, if desired, with avocado slices. Serve with cut corn. Refrigerate leftovers. 6 to 8 servings.

Mirlet TerMaat, Wisconsin

COUNTRY STYLE CHICKEN KIEV

½ cup fine dry bread crumbs
2 tablespoons grated Parmesan cheese
1 teaspoon dried basil leaves
1 teaspoon dried oregano leaves
½ teaspoon garlic salt
¼ teaspoon salt, if desired
6 to 8 SCHWAN'S Unbreaded Chicken Breast Filets, thawed
⅔ cup butter, melted
¼ cup dry white wine
¼ cup chopped green onions
¼ cup chopped fresh parsley

Heat oven to 375°F. On waxed paper, combine bread crumbs, Parmesan cheese, basil, oregano, garlic salt and salt. Dip chicken in melted butter and roll in crumbs to coat. Place chicken in 13x9-inch pan. Bake at 375°F. for 45 to 50 minutes, or until golden brown and chicken is no longer pink inside.

Meanwhile, in small bowl, combine wine, onions, parsley and remaining melted butter; mix and pour over chicken. Bake for 3 to 5 minutes, or until sauce is hot. Serve sauce spooned over chicken. Refrigerate leftovers. 6 to 8 servings.

Schwan's TIP

Q: What is the general rule for adding fresh herbs to a recipe?

A: If you're experimenting with fresh herbs, start by adding about 1 teaspoon of herb for each 4 servings. If you want a stronger flavor, add more of the herb gradually, tasting as you go, until you are satisfied.

MaryLou Tease, Ohio

LEMONADE CHICKEN

- **½ cup SCHWAN'S Lemonade Concentrate, thawed**
- **3 tablespoons soy sauce**
- **¼ teaspoon celery salt**
- **⅛ teaspoon garlic powder**
- **6 SCHWAN'S Unbreaded Chicken Breast Filets, thawed**

In small bowl, mix together lemonade concentrate, soy sauce, celery salt and garlic powder; reserve 3 tablespoons for basting chicken during cooking. In large plastic bag, place chicken; pour in lemon mixture. Refrigerate 1 hour, turning occasionally.

Grill or broil about 4 to 6 minutes per side, or until chicken is no longer pink inside, basting with reserved marinade once or twice. Refrigerate leftovers. 6 servings.

Lemonade Chicken with QUIK TATER Packets p.59

Jacquie Clingan, Illinois

CHICKEN A L'ORANGE

- **½ cup prepared SCHWAN'S Orange Juice**
- **1 tablespoon soy sauce**
- **4 SCHWAN'S Unbreaded Chicken Breast Filets, thawed**
- **4 teaspoons orange marmalade**

In shallow dish, mix orange juice and soy sauce; add chicken, turning to coat thoroughly. Cover and refrigerate for at least 1 hour, turning chicken once.

Heat oven to 325°F. Place chicken and orange juice mixture in a 9-inch square pan; top each chicken breast with 1 teaspoon orange marmalade. Bake, uncovered, at 325°F. for 30 to 35 minutes or until chicken is no longer pink inside. Refrigerate leftovers. 4 servings.

Mary Picchietti, Illinois

BREADED CHICKEN BREAST FILETS IN TOMATO SAUCE

2 tablespoons oil
2 cups chopped onions
1 (29-oz.) can tomato puree
1 cup water
1 teaspoon dried oregano leaves
1 to 2 teaspoons salt, if desired
½ to 1 teaspoon pepper
1 (2.25-lb.) box SCHWAN'S Breaded Chicken Breast Filets
2 cups GOURMET'S CHOICE Green Peas
Cooked pasta or GOURMET'S CHOICE Italian Pasta Blend, if desired

Heat oil in 4½ to 5-quart Dutch oven; sauté onions until tender. Add tomato puree, water, oregano, salt and pepper. Bring to a boil; reduce heat and simmer 10 to 15 minutes, stirring occasionally. Add chicken, covering with sauce; cover and simmer 15 minutes, rearranging chicken occasionally to heat evenly. Add peas; cover and simmer 10 minutes. Serve on pasta or GOURMET'S CHOICE Italian Pasta Blend, if desired. Refrigerate leftovers. 8 to 10 servings.

Sandra Bengtson, Minnesota

ITALIAN CHICKEN & CHEESE

4 SCHWAN'S Breaded Chicken Breast Filets
½ cup tomato sauce
¼ teaspoon Italian seasoning
Salt, to taste
Pepper, to taste
2 (4x4-inch) slices mozzarella cheese, cut into 4 pieces
2 slices SCHWAN'S American Processed Cheese, cut into 4 pieces

Heat oven to 425°F. Arrange filets, sides touching, in ungreased 9-inch square pan; bake, uncovered, at 425°F. for 20 minutes, or until hot.

Remove from oven; cover filets with tomato sauce, sprinkle with Italian seasoning, salt and pepper. Dividing cheese evenly, layer mozzarella and American cheese on each filet. Bake, uncovered, at 425°F. for 5 minutes, or until cheese is melted. Refrigerate leftovers. 4 servings.

Phyllis Hering, Illinois

SPICY CHICKEN

4 SCHWAN'S Breaded Chicken Breast Patties
6 tablespoons salsa
½ cup shredded mozzarella cheese

In 9-inch square microwave-safe dish, place chicken. Microwave on HIGH for 2½ to 3 minutes. Spoon 1½ tablespoons salsa on each patty; sprinkle each with 2 tablespoons cheese. Microwave on HIGH for 30 to 60 seconds or until cheese is melted. 4 servings.

NOTE: Microwave timings are for 700 to 800 watt microwave ovens. With an oven of different wattage output, timings may need slight adjustment.

Cheryl Oblick, Pennsylvania

TURKEY CACCIATORE

2 teaspoons olive oil
4 LORI'S KITCHEN Unbreaded Turkey Breast Filets
1 cup sliced onions
1 (29-oz.) can (3½ cups) tomato sauce
1 teaspoon dried oregano leaves
8 cups GOURMET'S CHOICE Summer Garden Pasta Blend

Heat oil in large nonstick skillet over medium heat; sauté turkey and onions for 7 to 9 minutes, turning turkey occasionally. Remove turkey from skillet; add tomato sauce, oregano and pasta blend to skillet. Arrange turkey on top and cook 10 to 15 minutes, stirring occasionally, until heated through. Refrigerate leftovers. 4 servings.

An "antique" ice cream maker from a bygone era. That same homemade-like ice cream is still available from Schwan's today.

Darlene Mann, Texas

TURKEY MARSALA

1 cup finely crushed saltine cracker crumbs
½ cup grated Parmesan cheese
1 tablespoon minced fresh parsley
½ teaspoon salt-free seasoning
½ teaspoon garlic powder
½ teaspoon paprika
⅛ teaspoon coarsely ground black pepper
⅔ cup water, divided
6 LORI'S KITCHEN Unbreaded Turkey Breast Filets, thawed
½ cup margarine, melted
⅓ cup Marsala wine

Heat oven to 350°F. In plastic bag, combine crumbs, Parmesan cheese, parsley, salt-free seasoning, garlic powder, paprika and pepper; set aside. Place ⅓ cup water in shallow dish; dip turkey breast filets into water and shake in crumb mixture. Spray a 13x9-inch pan with nonstick cooking spray; add remaining ⅓ cup water. Place filets in pan and drizzle with margarine. Bake, uncovered, at 350°F. for 20 minutes.

Reduce oven temperature to 325°F. Pour wine over turkey; cover with foil and bake for 10 minutes. Remove foil and continue baking for 5 minutes. Refrigerate leftovers. 4 to 6 servings.

Alice Holman, North Dakota

TURKEY FILETS SUPREME

6 LORI'S KITCHEN Unbreaded Turkey Breast Filets, thawed
2 tablespoons margarine or butter, melted
2 tablespoons chopped fresh parsley
2 tablespoons chopped onions
¼ cup flour
1 egg, lightly beaten
⅔ cup cracker crumbs
½ cup sherry wine
½ cup margarine or butter, melted

Heat oven to 350°F. Flatten turkey breasts by placing between pieces of wax paper and pounding with rolling pin or meat mallet. Spread 2 tablespoons margarine on filets; sprinkle with parsley and onions. Roll up; secure with toothpicks. Roll in flour, dip in egg and roll in crumbs. Place in 8-inch square baking pan. In small bowl, mix together wine and ½ cup margarine; pour over turkey. Cover and bake at 350°F. for 40 minutes; uncover and continue baking for 20 minutes. Refrigerate leftovers. 6 servings.

Bill Boyd, Pennsylvania

ORANGE TURKEY BREASTS

1 egg, lightly beaten
⅓ cup prepared SCHWAN'S Orange Juice Concentrate
1½ cups stuffing mix
1 tablespoon grated orange peel
1 teaspoon paprika
¼ to ½ teaspoon salt
8 LORI'S KITCHEN Unbreaded Turkey Breast Filets
6 tablespoons butter, melted
Orange slices, if desired

Heat oven to 375°F. In shallow dish, mix together egg and orange juice; set aside. On waxed paper, mix together stuffing mix, orange peel, paprika and salt. Dip turkey breasts into egg mixture, then into crumb mixture. Melt butter in 13x9-inch pan in oven. Turn coated turkey breasts in butter to coat both sides.

Bake, uncovered, at 375°F. for 45 minutes or until turkey is no longer pink inside. Garnish with orange slices, if desired. Refrigerate leftovers. 6 to 8 servings.

Orange Turkey Breasts

Ann Chontos, North Dakota

BEEF STIR-FRY

- 2 to 3 HAUGIN'S PRIDE Sirloin Ball Tip Steaks
- 1 tablespoon olive oil
- 2 garlic cloves, crushed
- Salt, to taste
- Pepper, to taste
- 5 cups GOURMET'S CHOICE Stir-Fry Vegetables
- ¼ cup reduced-calorie Italian salad dressing
- 1 tablespoon grated Parmesan cheese
- Cooked pasta

Cut steaks into ⅛ to ¼-inch strips. Heat oil in large (12-inch) nonstick skillet or wok over medium-high heat; add garlic, cook 1 minute. Add ½ of the steak, stir-fry for 1 to 2 minutes; season with salt and pepper. Remove steak, keep warm. Stir-fry remaining ½ of the steak; season with salt and pepper. Remove steak; keep warm. Add vegetables to skillet; stir-fry for 2 to 3 minutes, or until crisply tender. Return steak to skillet; add Italian dressing, cooking and stirring until heated through.

Sprinkle with Parmesan cheese and serve over pasta. Refrigerate leftovers. 4 servings.

TIPS: 4 or 5 SCHWAN'S Unbreaded Chicken Breast Filets may be substituted for steaks.

Serve with LORI'S KITCHEN 5-Cheese Garlic French Bread.

Sarah Smith, North Carolina

BEEF & SPINACH STIR-FRY

- 4 (4-oz.) HAUGIN'S PRIDE Sirloin Filet Beef Steaks
- 3 tablespoons sherry wine
- 2 tablespoons soy sauce
- ½ teaspoon sesame oil
- 10 cups (2-lb. pkg.) GOURMET'S CHOICE Cut Leaf Spinach
- 1 teaspoon grated gingerroot
- 3 tablespoons peanut oil, divided
- 2 tablespoons water
- 1 teaspoon chicken bouillon granules
- ½ teaspoon cornstarch
- Cooked GOURMET'S CHOICE IQF White Rice

Cut steak into thin strips; set aside.

In medium bowl, combine sherry, soy sauce and sesame oil; mix well. Stir in steak; cover, refrigerate for 2 hours. Rinse spinach to thaw; drain well and pat dry. Heat 2 tablespoons oil in wok or large (12-inch) skillet over high heat. Stir-fry spinach and ginger for 2 minutes; remove from skillet. Add remaining 1 tablespoon oil to skillet; drain steak, reserve marinade. Stir-fry steak a few pieces at a time for 3 minutes or until done. Remove steak; keep warm.

In small bowl, mix water, bouillon, cornstarch and reserved marinade; add to wok, cook and stir for 1 to 2 minutes or until boiling. Return spinach and steak to wok and continue stir-frying 2 minutes or until heated through. Serve with rice. Refrigerate leftovers. 4 to 6 servings.

Beef Stir-Fry

Marion Skager, North Dakota

QUICK BEEF STIR-FRY FOR 2

2 tablespoons oil
2 HAUGIN'S PRIDE Floured Cubed Beef Steaks
2 cups GOURMET'S CHOICE Stir-Fry Vegetables
2 tablespoons stir-fry sauce, if desired
Cooked GOURMET'S CHOICE IQF White Rice OR Cooked LORI'S KITCHEN Cheese Tortellini

Heat oil in medium (10-inch) skillet over medium heat. Cut steaks into 1-inch cubes and cook until browned, about 2 minutes. Add vegetables and stir-fry 4 to 5 minutes. Add stir-fry sauce, if desired. Serve over rice or cheese tortellini. Refrigerate leftovers. 2 servings.

Carolyn Johnson, Oklahoma

MEXICAN STIR-FRY

2 (6-oz.) HAUGIN'S PRIDE Sirloin Ball Tip Steaks
1 tablespoon taco seasoning
1 tablespoon oil
1½ cups GOURMET'S CHOICE Stir-Fry Vegetables
¾ cup salsa
8 tortillas, heated
1 cup shredded Cheddar cheese
Shredded lettuce
Dairy sour cream

Cut steaks into 2x½-inch strips; sprinkle with taco seasoning. In medium (10-inch) nonstick skillet, heat oil and stir-fry steak until no longer pink; remove and set aside. Add vegetables and salsa to skillet; cook and stir 3 to 5 minutes or until hot. Add steak to vegetable mixture and heat thoroughly.

Serve on tortillas topped with Cheddar cheese, lettuce and sour cream, or roll up and serve with additional salsa. Refrigerate leftovers. 4 to 6 servings.

The foundation of SCHWAN'S Home Food Service was built on the dairy business in Minnesota. For many years the family dairy fulfilled the milk needs of Marshall and surrounding communities.

Jody Courtney, Montana

AMERICAN BEEF STIR-FRY

1 cup water
½ cup soy sauce
2 tablespoons cornstarch
3 tablespoons oil
½ cup chopped green bell pepper
⅓ cup chopped onions
2 HAUGIN'S PRIDE Sirloin Filet Beef Steaks, thinly sliced
5 cups GOURMET'S CHOICE California Blend
1 teaspoon garlic powder
Salt, to taste
Pepper, to taste
3 cups cooked brown rice

In small bowl, combine water, soy sauce and cornstarch; set aside. Heat oil in large (12-inch) skillet over medium-high heat. Add bell pepper and onions; cook and stir until tender. Add steak; stir-fry until no longer pink, about 2 minutes. Add vegetables, stir-fry until tender-crisp, about 4 to 5 minutes; sprinkle with garlic powder. Reduce heat to low; stir in cornstarch mixture. Cook, stirring constantly, 2 minutes or until thickened and bubbly. Add salt and pepper to taste. Serve over rice. Refrigerate leftovers. 4 servings.

Schwan's TIP

Q: Can cornstarch be substituted for flour as a thickener?

A: Yes. Cornstarch has twice the thickening power of flour, so when substituting cornstarch for flour, use half as much cornstarch.

Nellie Ann Bush, Michigan

WOK ITALIAN

- 3 to 4 HAUGIN'S PRIDE BIG SAM Sirloin Steaks
- 3 tablespoons low-sodium soy sauce
- 2 tablespoons water
- 1 tablespoon cornstarch
- 1 teaspoon sugar
- ⅛ teaspoon garlic powder
- ⅛ teaspoon coarsely ground black pepper
- 1 pound spaghetti
- 2 tablespoons olive oil or oil, divided
- 5 tablespoons Chinese oyster sauce, divided
- 5½ cups GOURMET'S CHOICE Stir-Fry Vegetables
- LORI'S KITCHEN 5-Cheese Garlic French Bread
- Sliced tomatoes

Partially thaw steaks; slice thinly across grain. In medium glass bowl, combine soy sauce, water, cornstarch, sugar, garlic powder and pepper; add beef, cover and refrigerate 1 to 2 hours.

When ready for meal, cook spaghetti according to package directions, adding 1 tablespoon oil to cooking water; drain. Stir in 2 tablespoons oyster sauce; keep warm.

Place remaining 1 tablespoon oil in wok or large (12-inch) skillet. Stir-fry undrained steak over medium heat for 3 to 5 minutes or until no longer pink. Push steak to sides; add vegetables and stir-fry 3 to 5 minutes or until tender-crisp. Stir together steak, vegetables and remaining 3 tablespoons oyster sauce. Reduce heat, partially cover and cook 1 minute.

Toss with warm spaghetti in serving bowl. Serve with LORI'S KITCHEN 5-Cheese Garlic French Bread and sliced tomatoes. Refrigerate leftovers. 6 servings.

Nancee Cope, South Carolina

NANCEE'S MARINATED STEAKS

- ½ cup white vinegar
- ½ cup soy sauce
- 1 tablespoon garlic powder
- 2 to 6 HAUGIN'S PRIDE BIG SAM Sirloin Steaks, thawed

In shallow glass dish large enough to hold steaks, combine vinegar, soy sauce and garlic powder; mix well. Add steaks, cover and refrigerate no more than 2 hours, turning occasionally.

Grill over medium heat for 20 minutes, for medium, turning once. Refrigerate leftovers. 2 to 6 servings.

TIP: Marinade can be used with SCHWAN'S Unbreaded Chicken Breast Filets. Marinate in the refrigerator for 15 to 30 minutes.

"I am a working mother with four beautiful children and I'm hooked on Schwan's! You have made my life so much easier. Now, no one complains that there's nothing to eat for supper. Goodbye canned soup and sandwiches."

Nancee Cope

Nancee's Marinated Steaks

Mary Alice DuBord, Indiana

CHEESY BEEF PASTA & VEGETABLES

- 2 (4-oz.) HAUGIN'S PRIDE Floured Cubed Beef Steaks
- 1½ cups GOURMET'S CHOICE Summer Garden Pasta Blend, thawed
- 1 (16-oz.) tub LORI'S KITCHEN Wisconsin Cheese Deli Soup, thawed
- 12 GOURMET'S CHOICE Breaded Onion Rings

Heat oven to 350°F. Spray medium (10-inch) skillet with nonstick cooking spray. Cook steaks 3 to 4 minutes or until brown; place in greased 1½-quart casserole. Add vegetables; top with soup. Cover; bake at 350°F. for 30 minutes. Remove cover; top with onion rings. Bake, uncovered, for 10 to 20 minutes or until bubbly in center and onion rings are crisp. Refrigerate leftovers. 4 servings.

Schwan's TIP

Pasta Pointers

When cooking homemade or commercially prepared frozen pasta, plan on 4 ounces for each main-dish serving and 2 ounces for each side-dish serving. When cooking packaged dried pasta, use 2 ounces for each main-dish serving and 1 ounce for each side-dish serving. Follow manufacturer's cooking instructions on the package. Pasta should be cooked in plenty of boiling water until it is just firm to the bite (al dente). Overcooking turns pasta into a soft and soggy mass.

Deb Mennis, North Dakota

DEB'S CHEESY BEEF CASSEROLE

- 4 cups GOURMET'S CHOICE QUIK TATERS
- 4 HAUGIN'S PRIDE Beef Patties
- 1 (16-oz.) tub LORI'S KITCHEN Wisconsin Cheese Deli Soup, thawed
- 1 cup GOURMET'S CHOICE Cut Corn, cooked
- 2 teaspoons finely chopped onions
- 4 slices SCHWAN'S American Processed Cheese

Heat oven to 350°F. Spray a 13x9-inch pan with nonstick cooking spray; spread Quik Taters in pan. Bake at 350°F. for 10 to 20 minutes.

In medium (10-inch) skillet, brown and crumble beef patties; drain. Add soup, corn and onions; stir and cook 4 to 5 minutes or until heated through.

Remove potatoes from oven; spoon meat mixture over potatoes. Cut cheese slices diagonally; place on soup mixture. Broil 2 to 5 minutes or until cheese melts. Let stand 5 minutes before cutting into squares to serve. Refrigerate leftovers. 6 servings.

Julie Gallagher, Texas

BBQ BEEF PIE

- 2 tablespoons butter or margarine
- 1 to 1½ cups (2 stalks) chopped celery with leaves
- ½ cup (1 medium) chopped onions
- 1½ pounds (1 tray) HAUGIN'S PRIDE Chopped BBQ Beef with Sauce, thawed
- 1 (16-oz.) can tomatoes, undrained and cut up
- 1 beef bouillon cube
- ½ teaspoon dried thyme leaves
- ½ teaspoon ground allspice
- ¼ teaspoon pepper
- 2 tablespoons fine dry bread crumbs
- 2 tablespoons chopped fresh parsley
- Pastry for 2-crust 9-inch deep-dish pie or 10-inch pie
- 1 egg, slightly beaten

Heat oven to 400°F. Melt butter in medium (10-inch) skillet; sauté celery and onions for 3 to 4 minutes, or until tender. Add beef, tomatoes, bouillon cube, thyme, allspice and pepper; lower heat and simmer 15 minutes. Remove from heat; stir in bread crumbs and parsley.

Place meat mixture in prepared pie crust, adjust top crust, cut vent holes and crimp edges. Brush top with egg. Bake at 400°F. for 35 to 40 minutes. Let stand for 10 minutes before cutting. Refrigerate leftovers.
6 to 8 servings.

JoAnn Stearns, South Dakota

BEEF POT PIE

- 1 (9-inch) pastry for 2-crust pie
- 1 (1½-lb.) bag HAUGIN'S PRIDE Beef Tips & Gravy, thawed
- ⅔ cup (1 medium) peeled and chopped potato
- ½ cup GOURMET'S CHOICE Cut Corn, thawed
- ½ cup GOURMET'S CHOICE Cut Green Beans, thawed
- ½ cup GOURMET'S CHOICE Green Peas, thawed
- ½ cup GOURMET'S CHOICE Baby Carrots, thawed and sliced
- ½ cup (1 medium) chopped onions

Heat oven to 375°F. Line 9-inch pie pan with crust. In medium bowl, mix beef tips and all vegetables. Put into crust; adjust top crust, cut vent holes and crimp edges.

Bake at 375°F. for 60 to 65 minutes or until top is golden brown. Let stand 10 minutes before cutting. Refrigerate leftovers.
6 servings.

Neva Thomas, Virginia

STEAK & PINEAPPLE KABOBS

4 HAUGIN'S PRIDE Sirloin Filet Beef Steaks
½ cup VITA-SUN Cranberry Apple Juice Drink Concentrate
½ cup soy sauce
2 tablespoons olive oil
1 tablespoon honey
½ teaspoon ground ginger
12 very small red-skinned potatoes
2 medium green bell peppers, each cut into 8 pieces
16 cherry tomatoes
16 pineapple chunks
8 skewers

Partially thaw steaks; cut each into 4 pieces, set aside. In shallow glass pan, mix cranberry apple juice drink concentrate, soy sauce, oil, honey and ginger; reserve ½ cup to baste kabobs during grilling. Place steak in mixture; marinate 1 hour, stirring occasionally.

Remove steak from marinade; discard marinade.

Heat grill. When ready to grill, alternately thread 4 pieces of steak and 3 potatoes, starting with steak, on 4 skewers. Leave a small space between pieces. Alternately thread bell peppers, tomatoes and pineapple on 4 additional skewers; set aside.

Grill steak and potato kabobs for 6 minutes, turning and brushing several times with reserved marinade. After 6 minutes, place vegetable kabobs on grill. Grill 5 to 6 minutes, turning several times and brushing all kabobs with reserved marinade. Refrigerate leftovers. 4 servings.

TIP: Partially cook potatoes, if desired.

Steak & Pineapple Kabobs

Kelly Difrisco, Tennessee

ITALIAN STYLE BROILED STEAK

¼ cup olive oil
2 tablespoons lemon juice
1 tablespoon dried oregano leaves
3 garlic cloves, crushed
½ teaspoon salt
¼ teaspoon pepper
4 HAUGIN'S PRIDE BIG SAM Sirloin Steaks

In small bowl, combine olive oil, lemon juice, oregano, garlic, salt and pepper; mix well. Reserve 2 tablespoons for basting steak during broiling. Place steaks in shallow glass dish, pour marinade over; refrigerate for 2 to 3 hours, turning occasionally. Remove steaks from marinade; discard marinade.

Heat broiler. Broil steaks 4 to 5 inches from heat for 8 minutes. Baste steak with reserved marinade and turn over. Continue cooking until done as desired, 7 to 10 minutes longer for medium. 4 servings.

TIP: Serve with prepared GOURMET'S CHOICE Summer Garden Pasta Blend, if desired.

Sis Rich, Texas

SCHWAN'S MEAL

1 teaspoon olive or vegetable oil
1 HAUGIN'S PRIDE Floured Cubed Beef Steak
1 GOURMET'S CHOICE Shredded Hashbrown portion
1 or 2 GOURMET'S CHOICE Breaded Onion Rings
¼ to ⅓ cup LORI'S KITCHEN Cream of Broccoli Soup or LORI'S KITCHEN Wisconsin Cheese Deli Soup

Heat oven to 350°F. Heat oil in small skillet. Add steak, *lightly brown* on both sides, about 3 minutes; remove and place on 10x18-inch piece of foil. In same skillet, slowly cook hashbrowns and onion rings for 2 to 3 minutes. Layer hashbrowns and onion rings on steak; top with soup. Seal foil securely. Bake at 350°F. for 1 hour. 1 serving.

TIP: More than one packet can be made; place packets on a cookie sheet for baking.

By the 1950's Schwan's had already established a tradition of producing the finest ice cream available anywhere.

Susan Vaillancourt, Oregon

CHOPS-N-RICE

4 HAUGIN'S FARM BRAND Center Cut Pork Loin Chops
5 cups GOURMET'S CHOICE IQF White Rice
1 cup chopped green onions
2 (4-oz.) cans sliced mushrooms, drained
¼ cup finely diced carrots
¼ cup low-sodium soy sauce

GLAZE
2 tablespoons low-sodium soy sauce
2 teaspoons water
1 teaspoon honey

Heat oven to 375°F. In medium (10-inch) skillet, brown pork chops. Prepare rice as directed on package; set aside. In small bowl, combine glaze ingredients; set aside.

In 2 to 2½-quart casserole, combine rice, onions, mushrooms and carrots; stir in ¼ cup soy sauce. Brush pork chops on all sides with glaze; place on top of rice mixture.

Bake at 375°F., uncovered, for 35 to 45 minutes or until chops are no longer pink, brushing once or twice with glaze. 4 servings

Schwan's TIP

Q: Can wooden skewers be used to cook kabobs on a grill?

A: Yes. Soak the skewers in water for a few minutes before you start threading the kabobs. This way the skewers won't burn as the food cooks. To make sure all items on a kabob are cooked evenly, thread the pieces loosely onto the skewers, leaving at least ¼ inch between pieces.

Betty Overdorf, Indiana

APPLE-STUFFED PORK CHOPS

6 HAUGIN'S FARM BRAND Center Cut Pork Loin Chops
¼ cup margarine
⅓ cup chopped celery
⅓ cup chopped onions
2¼ cups soft bread crumbs
1 cup peeled and chopped apple
½ teaspoon salt
¼ teaspoon rubbed sage
¼ teaspoon dried parsley leaves
⅛ teaspoon pepper
2 tablespoons vegetable oil
¼ cup prepared VITA-SUN Apple Juice Drink

Cut pockets in chops with sharp knife; set aside. Heat margarine in medium (10-inch) skillet over medium heat; add celery and onions and cook until tender. Remove from heat; stir in bread crumbs, apple, salt, sage, parsley and pepper. Stuff pork chops with bread crumb mixture; fasten with toothpicks. Heat oil in large (12-inch) skillet over medium heat; brown chops about 15 minutes and drain. Add apple juice drink; cover, lower heat and simmer 1 hour. Refrigerate leftovers. 6 servings.

Marla Galbreath, Illinois

PORK CHOPS O'BRIAN

1 tablespoon oil
6 HAUGIN'S FARM BRAND Center Cut Pork Loin Chops
1 (16-oz.) tub LORI'S KITCHEN Cream of Broccoli Soup, thawed
½ cup milk or dairy sour cream
½ teaspoon salt
½ teaspoon pepper
9 GOURMET'S CHOICE Shredded Hashbrowns, thawed and crumbled
6 slices SCHWAN'S American Processed Cheese, diced and divided
1 (2.8-oz.) can French-fried onions

Heat oven to 350°F. Heat oil in large (12-inch) skillet; brown chops on both sides. Drain; set aside. In large bowl, combine soup, milk, salt and pepper; mix well. Stir in potatoes, ½ of cheese and ½ of onions. Spoon mixture into greased 13x9-inch baking dish; arrange chops on top.

Cover with foil; bake at 350°F. for 40 minutes. Remove cover; sprinkle with remaining cheese and onions. Bake, uncovered, 5 to 10 minutes. 6 servings.

Schwan's TIP

Q: What is the best way to thaw meat?

A: Thaw frozen meat in the refrigerator overnight. For faster thawing, use a microwave oven following oven manufacturer's directions. Do not thaw meat at room temperature.

Pork Chops O'Brian

Bernice Smith, Oklahoma

CORN DOG DIPPING SAUCE

¼ cup vegetable oil
2 cups finely chopped onions
1¼ cup catsup
½ cup water
¼ cup firmly packed brown sugar
1 tablespoon red wine vinegar
1 teaspoon prepared mustard
½ to 1 teaspoon salt
SCHWAN'S Corn Dogs, prepared

Heat oil in medium saucepan; add onions and cook until tender. Add remaining ingredients; simmer uncovered 15 minutes. Serve with SCHWAN'S Corn Dogs.
3 cups sauce.

Beth Johnson, Michigan

HOT DOG BAR-B-Q

10 (1 lb.) HAUGIN'S PRIDE Skinless Franks
1 tablespoon oil
⅔ cup chopped onions
1 (14-oz.) bottle chili sauce
2 tablespoons hamburger pickle relish
1 tablespoon sugar
1 tablespoon vinegar
¼ teaspoon salt
⅛ teaspoon pepper
10 toasted hot dog buns

Score franks by making slanted cuts ¼ of the way through frank and about 1 inch apart. Heat oil in medium (10-inch) skillet; cook onions until tender. *Do not* brown. Stir in chili sauce, pickle relish, sugar, vinegar, salt and pepper; add franks. Simmer about 10 minutes, stirring occasionally. Serve on toasted buns. Refrigerate leftovers.
8 to 10 servings.

Lori McCarty, Indiana

BRATWURST HOT DISH

10 GOURMET'S CHOICE Shredded Hashbrowns
2 (16-oz.) cans sauerkraut, drained
½ cup firmly packed brown sugar
1½ pounds (7 to 8) HAUGIN'S FARM BRAND Bratwurst, cut into 1-inch pieces

Heat oven to 350°F. Spray 13x9-inch pan with nonstick cooking spray. Line bottom of prepared pan with hashbrowns; spread with sauerkraut and sprinkle with brown sugar. Top with bratwurst.

Bake at 350°F. for 1¼ to 1½ hours, or until bratwurst is golden brown. Refrigerate leftovers. 6 to 8 servings.

Barbara Sutton, Tennessee

BREAKFAST BURRITOS

10 HAUGIN'S FARM BRAND Pork Sausage Patties, thawed
½ cup diced onions
2 GOURMET'S CHOICE Shredded Hashbrowns, thawed and crumbled
6 eggs, lightly beaten
6 to 8 (8 to 10-inch) flour tortillas, heated
Picante sauce
Shredded Cheddar cheese

In large (12-inch) skillet, cook sausage and onions over medium heat until sausage is no longer pink; drain. Add hashbrowns and eggs; stir and cook until eggs are set.

Spoon filling into heated tortillas. Serve with picante sauce and shredded cheese. Refrigerate leftovers. 6 to 8 servings.

Schwan's TIP

Q: Why should metal containers be avoided for use in marinating foods?

A: The acid in the marinade may pit the container. The pitting not only ruins the container, but it also may add an off flavor to the marinade. To reduce cleanup, use a plastic bag set in a bowl to hold the food you are marinating. Seal the bag and turn it occasionally to distribute the mixture over the food. To be sure your marinated foods are safe to eat, do not marinate them at room temperature for more than 1 hour. If a recipe calls for a longer marinating time, refrigerate the marinating food.

Linda Risk, Wisconsin

EASY CHEESY POTATO & HAM CASSEROLE

1 (8-oz.) package shredded Cheddar cheese, divided
1 (16-oz.) tub LORI'S KITCHEN Wisconsin Cheese Deli Soup, thawed
1 cup finely chopped onions
2 cups cubed HAUGIN'S FARM BRAND Ham
1 (1½-lb.) bag GOURMET'S CHOICE QUIK TATERS, thawed

Heat oven to 325°F. Grease 13x9-inch pan. Measure ½ cup cheese; set aside. In large bowl, mix remaining cheese, soup and onions; stir in ham. Gently stir in QUIK TATERS. Pour mixture into prepared pan. Cover with foil and bake at 325°F. for 1 hour. Remove foil; sprinkle with reserved cheese. Bake, uncovered, for 15 minutes. Refrigerate leftovers. 6 to 8 servings.

Schwan's TIP

Handy Ham Tips

Combine strips of ham with vegetables or fruit for a quick salad or fancy hors-d' oeuvre. Use in your favorite classic casserole or soup recipe. A slice of ham adds the finishing touch to any sandwich, hot or cold.

Paula Curtis, Pennsylvania

CHEESE TORTELLINI & HAM BAKE

2 (16-oz.) tubs LORI'S KITCHEN Wisconsin Cheese Deli Soup, thawed
12 to 14 GOURMET'S CHOICE Broccoli Spears, thawed and cut into large pieces
6 cups LORI'S KITCHEN Cheese Tortellini
2 cups cubed HAUGIN'S FARM BRAND Ham
1 cup Italian seasoned fine dry bread crumbs
6 slices SCHWAN'S American Processed Cheese, cut into strips

Heat oven to 375°F. In large saucepan, combine soup and broccoli. Heat over medium heat for 5 to 10 minutes. Meanwhile, prepare tortellini according to package directions.

In a greased 2½ to 3-quart casserole, place tortellini. Spoon on soup mixture; top with ham and bread crumbs. Place cheese strips over bread crumbs. Bake at 375°F. for 20 to 25 minutes. Refrigerate leftovers. 4 to 6 servings.

TIP: Serve with GOURMET'S CHOICE Breaded Mushrooms or Seasoned Potato Curls.

Cynthia Prins, Pennsylvania

HAUGIN'S FARM HAM WITH ORANGE SAUCE

1 HAUGIN'S FARM BRAND Ham

ORANGE SAUCE

1 (9-oz.) jar orange marmalade
½ cup prepared SCHWAN'S Orange Juice
1 tablespoon prepared mustard
¼ teaspoon ground cloves
¼ teaspoon ground ginger
Whole cloves

Bake ham as directed on wrapper or until internal temperature reaches 140°F.

Meanwhile, in small saucepan, combine marmalade, orange juice, mustard, ground cloves and ginger. Simmer for 4 minutes, stirring occasionally; set aside. About ½ hour before ham is done, remove ham from oven. Turn oven to 350°F. Score ham with a sharp knife, cutting about ¼-inch deep. Spoon half of orange mixture over ham; stud with whole cloves. Bake at 350°F. for 30 minutes. Heat remaining sauce to serve with ham. Refrigerate leftovers. Makes 1⅓ cups of sauce.

Patricia Friend, New Jersey

SCHWAN'S BROCCOLI SURPRISE

½ cup butter or margarine
3 large GOURMET'S CHOICE Broccoli Spears, thawed and cut into 1-inch pieces
½ cup chopped onions
1 (16-oz.) tub LORI'S KITCHEN Cream of Broccoli Soup
2 cups cubed (½-inch) HAUGIN'S FARM BRAND Ham
½ cup uncooked long grain rice
½ cup shredded Cheddar cheese

Heat oven to 350°F. In 4-quart saucepan, melt butter; add broccoli and onions. Cook until tender; set aside. In 2½-quart casserole, mix together soup, broccoli and onions, ham and rice. Cover; bake at 350°F. for 30 minutes. Remove cover; stir. Bake additional 30 minutes; sprinkle with cheese. Refrigerate leftovers. 6 servings.

TIP: Serve with SCHWAN'S homemade bread, a garden salad and VITA-SUN Pineapple-Orange Drink.

"We've used SCHWAN'S products for years – since I was a teenager. We have always enjoyed the food and the service."

Patricia Friend

Cyndi Woodruff, North Carolina

BREAKFAST BAKE

12 eggs
1 cup milk
12 SCHWAN'S Shredded Hashbrowns, thawed and crumbled
2 cups chopped HAUGIN'S FARM BRAND Ham
1 cup shredded Cheddar cheese
½ cup chopped green bell pepper
½ cup chopped onions
½ to ¾ teaspoon salt
⅛ to ¼ teaspoon pepper

Heat oven to 325°F. In medium bowl, beat eggs and milk; set aside. Spray 13x9-inch baking pan with nonstick cooking spray. Mix together in prepared pan, hashbrowns, ham, cheese, bell pepper, onions, salt and pepper. Top with egg mixture. Bake at 325°F. for 60 to 75 minutes, or until eggs are set. Let stand 5 to 10 minutes before serving; cut into squares to serve. Refrigerate leftovers. 8 to 10 servings.

Carolyn Johnston, Idaho

BREAKFAST SKILLET

6 GOURMET'S CHOICE Shredded Hashbrowns
8 HAUGIN'S FARM BRAND Pork Sausage Links, browned and cut into ¼-inch pieces
1 cup chopped HAUGIN'S FARM BRAND Ham
¾ cup chopped onions
¾ cup chopped red bell pepper
¾ cup chopped green bell pepper
Salt, to taste
Pepper, to taste
6 eggs, slightly beaten
¼ to ½ teaspoon salt
¼ to ½ teaspoon pepper
2 cups shredded Cheddar cheese
Salsa, if desired

Spray large (12-inch) cast iron or heavy skillet with nonstick cooking spray. Heat hashbrowns, breaking apart. Add sausage, ham, onions and bell peppers; cook over medium-high heat until hashbrowns are light brown and onions and peppers are tender. Season to taste with salt and pepper. In medium bowl, mix eggs, ¼ to ½ teaspoon salt and ¼ to ½ teaspoon pepper. Pour eggs over hashbrown mixture; lower heat to medium. Cover; cook 5 minutes or until eggs are set. Remove cover; sprinkle with cheese. Cover and cook over low heat 5 minutes to melt cheese. Remove from heat; let stand 10 minutes before slicing into wedges. Serve with salsa if desired. Refrigerate leftovers. 8 to 10 servings.

Peach Streusel Coffee Cake (top) p.146
Breakfast Bake (bottom)

Mary Alice DuBord, Indiana

AU GRATIN POLISH SAUSAGE & VEGETABLES

- 2 HAUGIN'S PRIDE Polish Sausages, thawed and cut into ¼-inch pieces
- 1½ cups GOURMET'S CHOICE California Blend
- ½ cup water
- 2 slices SCHWAN'S American Processed Cheese

In 1½-quart microwave-safe casserole, place sausage, California Blend and water. Microwave on HIGH for 13 minutes, stirring after 7 minutes. Stir; place cheese slices on top. Microwave for 20 seconds. Cover; let stand 1 minute. Refrigerate leftovers. 2 servings.

NOTE: Microwave timings are for 700 to 800 watt microwave ovens. With an oven of different wattage output, timings may need slight adjustment.

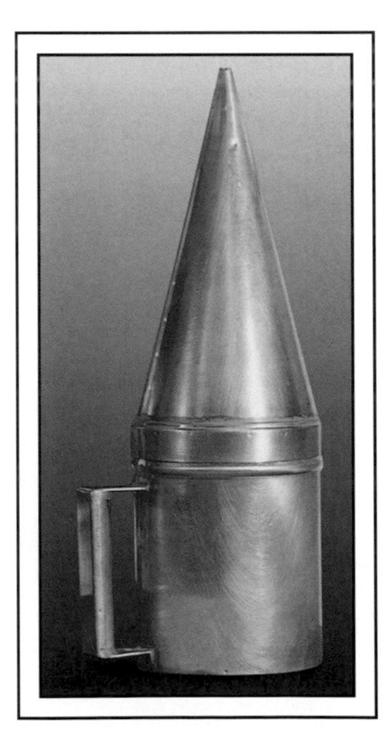

One of the first "rippler" devices used to produce the swirl in a wide variety of ice cream flavors.

Lorraine Baarson, Oregon

POLISH SAUSAGE & SAUERKRAUT

- ¼ cup butter
- 6 to 8 HAUGIN'S PRIDE Polish Sausage, thawed and cut into 2-inch pieces
- 1 large onion, sliced
- 1 (16-oz.) can sauerkraut, undrained
- 1 medium apple, peeled, cored and thinly sliced
- ½ cup dry white wine
- ½ cup water
- 2 tablespoons brown sugar
- 1 garlic clove, crushed
- 1 teaspoon salt
- ⅛ teaspoon pepper

Heat oven to 350°F. Melt butter in large (12-inch) skillet; sauté sausage and onions. Remove sausage from skillet. Add sauerkraut, apple, wine, water, brown sugar, garlic, salt and pepper to skillet; mix well. In an ungreased 1½-quart casserole, place sauerkraut mixture; top with sausage.

Bake, covered, at 350°F. for 1 hour. Refrigerate leftovers. 6 to 8 servings.

Alice Brekke, North Dakota

POLISH CHEESE POTATOES

1 (16-oz.) tub LORI'S KITCHEN Wisconsin Cheese Deli Soup, thawed
½ cup dairy sour cream
½ cup milk
¼ cup chopped onions
8 GOURMET'S CHOICE Shredded Hashbrowns
4 HAUGIN'S PRIDE Polish Sausage, thawed and cut into ⅛-inch slices
1 cup shredded Cheddar cheese

Heat oven to 375°F. Spray 13x9-inch baking dish with nonstick cooking spray. In medium bowl, combine soup, sour cream, milk and onions; mix well and set aside. Arrange hashbrowns in dish; top with sliced sausage. Pour soup mixture over sausage. Sprinkle with cheese.

Bake at 375°F. for 45 to 50 minutes. Refrigerate leftovers. 4 to 6 servings.

Neva Thomas, Virginia

SAUSAGE VEGETABLE PIZZA BAKE

10 cups (2 lb.) GOURMET'S CHOICE Italian Pasta Blend
8 HAUGIN'S FARM BRAND Pork Sausage Patties, thawed
2 (14-oz.) jars pizza sauce
1 (4-oz.) can sliced mushrooms, undrained
6 slices SCHWAN'S American Processed Cheese, cubed

Heat oven to 375°F. Thaw Italian Pasta Blend under cool running water in colander; set aside to drain. In large (12-inch) skillet, cook sausage, breaking each pattie into 4 or 5 pieces; drain. Remove half of cooked sausage; set aside. To remaining sausage in skillet, add pizza sauce and mushrooms with liquid. Stir and simmer 1 minute. Add Italian Pasta Blend and cheese; mix gently. Place mixture in greased 12x8-inch (2-quart) baking dish. Top with reserved sausage. Bake at 375°F. for 30 minutes. Refrigerate leftovers. 8 servings.

$1,000 Winner
Neva Thomas, Virginia

SANCHOS® WITH SWEET PEPPER SAUCE

6 slices HAUGIN'S FARM BRAND Thick Sliced Bacon, diced
1¼ cups (1 large) coarsely chopped onions
3 medium red bell peppers, cut into ¼-inch strips
3 medium yellow bell peppers, cut into ¼-inch strips
2 garlic cloves, minced
½ cup water
2 cups picante sauce
8 SCHWAN'S SANCHOS
8 slices SCHWAN'S American Processed Cheese

Heat oven to 375°F. Spray 13x9-inch pan with nonstick cooking spray; set aside. In large (12-inch) skillet, cook bacon and onions until bacon is crisp. Drain; reserve 2 tablespoons of drippings. Add peppers and garlic to skillet; sauté for 1 minute. Add water; cover and cook over medium heat 10 minutes, or until vegetables are tender. Stir in picante sauce; mix well. Place SANCHOS in prepared pan; top with cheese and sauce. Bake at 375°F. for 30 to 35 minutes. Refrigerate leftovers.
4 to 8 servings.

SANCHOS With Sweet Pepper Sauce

"I like to create recipes for SCHWAN'S products. First, I have an ingredient that I want to use. Then I build the flavors together in my mind to see what would be good together. Also, I look for nutritional balance in the ingredients."

Neva Thomas

Diane Davidson, Texas

SAUSAGE & RICE

8 HAUGIN'S FARM BRAND Pork Sausage Patties, thawed
⅔ cup chopped onions
1 (8-oz.) can or 2 (4-oz.) cans sliced mushrooms, drained
⅓ cup chopped red bell pepper
4 cups GOURMET'S CHOICE IQF White Rice
1 cup GOURMET'S CHOICE Green Peas
⅓ cup chicken broth
Salt, to taste

In large (12-inch) nonstick skillet over medium-high heat, crumble sausage and cook until no longer pink; drain, reserving 1 teaspoon drippings. Return sausage and reserved drippings to skillet; add onions, mushrooms and bell pepper. Sauté 4 to 5 minutes. Reduce heat to medium-low. Stir in rice, peas and broth; simmer 5 minutes. Add salt to taste and serve immediately. Refrigerate leftovers. 6 to 8 servings.

Mary Claire Hatlen, Wisconsin

QUIK TATER® SAUSAGE BAKE

½ cup (1 medium) chopped onions
8 HAUGIN'S FARM BRAND Pork Sausage Patties, thawed and crumbled
1 (16-oz.) tub LORI'S KITCHEN Wisconsin Cheese Deli Soup, thawed
1 (16-oz.) tub LORI'S KITCHEN Cream of Broccoli Soup, thawed
6 cups GOURMET'S CHOICE QUIK TATERS
2 to 3 GOURMET'S CHOICE Broccoli Spears, thawed and chopped
1 cup GOURMET'S CHOICE Cut Green Beans, thawed
Salt, to taste
Pepper, to taste

Heat oven to 350°F. In 4½ to 5-quart Dutch oven sauté onions and sausage. Cook 3 to 4 minutes, or until sausage is no longer pink; drain. Add thawed soups; stir in Quik Taters, broccoli and green beans. Season to taste with salt and pepper. Spoon into greased 3-quart casserole. Bake at 350°F. for 1 hour. Refrigerate leftovers. 6 to 8 servings.

Leslie Watson, Georgia

SUPREME FRIED RICE

2 tablespoons margarine
½ cup (about 4) sliced green onions
3 slices HAUGIN'S FARM BRAND Thick Sliced Bacon, diced
2 eggs, slightly beaten
1 cup cooked GOURMET'S CHOICE IQF White Rice
1 (8-oz.) can sliced water chestnuts, drained
1 (4-oz.) can sliced mushrooms, drained
1½ cups SEAFARER'S CHOICE P & D Shrimp, thawed
1 cup diced HAUGIN'S FARM BRAND Ham
1 cup SCHWAN'S Diced Chicken Meat, thawed
½ cup GOURMET'S CHOICE Green Peas, thawed
1 tablespoon soy sauce

Heat margarine in large (12-inch) skillet; sauté onions, remove and set aside. In same skillet, cook bacon until crisp; drain well, crumble and set aside. Over low heat, cook and stir eggs in bacon drippings until done; stir in rice, water chestnuts, mushrooms, shrimp, ham, chicken and peas; cook until heated through. Stir in soy sauce and sautéed onions; sprinkle with cooked bacon. Serve immediately. Refrigerate leftovers. 4 to 6 servings.

Supreme Fried Rice

Schwan's TIP

Food Safety?

- Maintain the refrigerator at 36°F. to 40°F. or below.
- Cook all foods thoroughly. Do not partially cook food, stop, and then finish cooking later.
- When serving hot foods, hold them for no longer than 2 hours and keep the food between 140°F. and 165°F. Throw away food that has been kept at room temperature for more than 2 hours.
- Promptly place leftovers in the refrigerator or freezer. A large quantity of hot food should be cooled quickly before refrigerating or freezing it. To do this, place the container in a sink filled with ice water. Or, divide the food into smaller portions before refrigerating or freezing, so it will cool faster.
- When handling raw meat or poultry, wash hands, counters, and utensils with hot, soapy water between recipe steps. Never put cooked meat or poultry on the plate that held the uncooked food.

Eleanor Emslie, North Dakota

CHILI BURRITO CASSEROLE

1 (15-oz.) can chili without beans
6 SCHWAN'S Burritos
1 cup shredded Cheddar cheese
¼ cup picante sauce
Dairy sour cream, if desired

Heat oven to 375°F. Spray 12x8-inch pan with nonstick cooking spray. In prepared pan, layer ½ of the chili, the burritos, remaining chili and cheese. Drizzle with picante sauce. Cover with foil and bake at 375°F. for 30 minutes. Serve hot. Garnish with dollops of sour cream, if desired. Refrigerate leftovers. 4 to 6 servings.

Joan Heaton, Indiania

QUICK CHIMICHANGA LUNCH

6 LORI'S KITCHEN Shredded Beef Chimichangas, partially thawed*
1½ cups GOURMET'S CHOICE Cut Corn
½ cup finely chopped green bell pepper
½ cup finely chopped red bell pepper
1 teaspoon chopped green chili peppers OR chopped jalapeño peppers
8 slices SCHWAN'S American Processed Cheese, cut into thin strips

Cut chimichangas into ½-inch pieces. In 2-quart microwave-safe casserole, place cut chimichangas, corn, green pepper, red pepper and chili peppers; stir gently. Microwave on HIGH 4 to 6 minutes or until hot, stirring once. Add cheese, stir and microwave on HIGH 1 to 2 minutes or until cheese is melted. Refrigerate leftovers. 4 to 6 servings.

*TIP: Chimichangas are easiest to cut when not completely thawed.

NOTE: Microwave timings are for 700 to 800 watt microwave ovens. With an oven of different wattage output, timings may need slight adjustment.

Quick Chimichanga Lunch

Café au lait
Mocha
Coffee

Mary Clare Hatlen, Wisconsin

SUNRISE BREAKFAST QUICHE

1 (9-inch) unbaked pie shell
3 eggs
½ cup milk
½ teaspoon dried minced onions
½ teaspoon salt
½ teaspoon pepper
1 (15-oz.) tray LORI'S KITCHEN Creamed Chipped Beef, thawed
4 GOURMET'S CHOICE Shredded Hashbrowns, thawed

Heat oven to 400°F. Prick pie crust and bake at 400°F. for 10 minutes; remove from oven. Reduce temperature to 350°F.

In large bowl, combine eggs, milk, onions, salt and pepper; beat until well blended. Fold in chipped beef and hashbrowns until well combined. Place pie pan on cookie sheet; spoon egg mixture into crust.

Bake at 350°F. for 30 to 45 minutes, or until a knife inserted halfway between center and edge comes out clean. Let stand 5 minutes before serving. Refrigerate leftovers.
6 to 8 servings.

Shelly Sanborn, Washington

PIEROGI KRAUT CASSEROLE

24 LORI'S KITCHEN Pierogies
4 slices HAUGIN'S FARM BRAND Thick Sliced Bacon, cut into 1-inch pieces
1 cup chopped onions
¼ cup sugar
¼ cup red wine vinegar
½ teaspoon caraway seed
½ teaspoon pepper
1 (16-oz.) can sauerkraut, drained
Dairy sour cream, if desired

Prepare pierogies as directed on package; drain and set aside. In large (12-inch) skillet, cook bacon until crisp; drain. Sauté onions in bacon drippings until tender. Add sugar, vinegar, caraway seed and pepper; simmer for 1 minute. Add pierogies, bacon and sauerkraut; mix gently and simmer for 10 minutes. Serve with sour cream, if desired. Refrigerate leftovers.
4 to 6 servings.

Honey Mixed Fruit Salad p.44
Sunrise Breakfast Quiche

Marvis Strickland, Texas

ROYAL CASSEROLE

12 LORI'S KITCHEN Pierogies
4 cups water
1 tablespoon lemon juice
1 teaspoon hot pepper sauce
5 cups (1 lb.) SEAFARER'S CHOICE P & D Shrimp, thawed
2 tablespoons butter, melted
1 cup GOURMET'S CHOICE Green Peas, thawed
1 (16-oz.) tub LORI'S KITCHEN Cream of Broccoli Soup, thawed
3 slices SCHWAN'S American Processed Cheese, diced

Heat oven to 350°F. Cook pierogies according to package directions. In large saucepan, bring water, lemon juice and hot pepper sauce to a boil; add shrimp. Cook 1 minute; drain.

Melt butter in 2-quart casserole. Place pierogies in casserole, turning to coat each with butter. Layer shrimp and peas on top of pierogies; pour soup over shrimp and peas. Sprinkle with cheese. Bake at 350°F. for 30 minutes. Refrigerate leftovers.
4 to 6 servings.

Sylvia Bronson, Montana

QUICK PIEROGI CASSEROLE

12 LORI'S KITCHEN Pierogies
3 tablespoons olive or vegetable oil
3 cups (8 oz.) thinly sliced fresh mushrooms
2 cups (2 large) thinly sliced onions
4 cups (5 large) diced plum tomatoes
1 cup water
1 tablespoon chopped parsley
¾ teaspoon salt
¼ teaspoon pepper

Heat oven to 350°F. Prepare pierogies as directed on package; drain. Heat oil in large (12-inch) skillet over medium heat; sauté mushrooms and onions until soft and golden. Add tomatoes, water, parsley, salt and pepper; heat to boiling. Boil 5 minutes. In 12x8-inch (2-quart) baking dish, arrange pierogies; cover with sauce. Cover with foil. Bake at 350°F. for 30 minutes, or until thoroughly heated. Refrigerate leftovers.
4 servings.

Quick Pierogi Casserole with Schwan's 5-Cheese Garlic French Bread

Sally Judge, Oklahoma

BAKED TORTELLINI & SPINACH

2 cups LORI'S KITCHEN Cheese Tortellini
2 cups SCHWAN'S Cut Leaf Spinach
1 cup ricotta cheese
1 egg, beaten
¼ teaspoon nutmeg
1 (26½-oz.) can spaghetti sauce
2 cups shredded mozzarella cheese
Water

Heat oven to 350°F. In microwave-safe casserole, place frozen tortellini; cover with water. Microwave on HIGH for 3 minutes; drain. Prepare spinach according to package directions; drain well. In small bowl, mix ricotta cheese, egg and nutmeg. In 9-inch square pan, spoon enough spaghetti sauce to cover bottom. Layer ½ of tortellini, ½ of spinach, ½ of ricotta mixture, 1 cup of mozzarella and ½ of remaining sauce; repeat layers. Cover and bake at 350°F. for 40 minutes. Refrigerate leftovers. 6 servings.

NOTE: Microwave timings are for 700 to 800 watt microwave ovens. With an oven of different wattage output, timings may need slight adjustment.

Yolanda Guenther, Michigan

WALNUT-TOPPED VEGETABLE CASSEROLE

12 cups water
5 cups GOURMET'S CHOICE Italian Pasta Blend
1 cup (4 oz.) fresh mushrooms, halved
2 tablespoons butter
2½ tablespoons flour
¾ cup milk
18 slices SCHWAN'S American Processed Cheese, quartered
1 cup plain yogurt
1 to 2 tablespoons fine dry bread crumbs
½ cup chopped walnuts

Heat oven to 350°F. In large saucepan, bring water to a boil; stir in Italian Pasta Blend and mushrooms. Cook for 2 minutes; drain and place in greased 2-quart casserole. Melt butter in small saucepan over low heat; add flour, stirring constantly. Gradually add milk; add cheese and stir until melted. Stir in yogurt and mix well; pour over vegetables. Sprinkle with bread crumbs and walnuts. Cover and bake at 350°F. for 30 minutes. Refrigerate leftovers. 4 to 6 servings.

TIP: Serve with LORI'S KITCHEN 5-Cheese Garlic French Bread, if desired.

Catherine Smith, Ohio

FLAUTA BREAKFAST CASSEROLE

- ⅓ cup margarine
- 14 SCHWAN'S Apple Flautas
- 4 eggs
- 1½ cups cups low-fat dairy sour cream
- ½ cup sugar
- 1 teaspoon vanilla
- 1 teaspoon almond extract

Heat oven to 350°F. Melt margarine in 13x9-inch pan. Arrange 2 columns of flautas over melted margarine. In medium bowl, whisk eggs for 1 minute; add sour cream, sugar, vanilla and almond extract; whisk until well blended. Pour over flautas. Bake at 350°F. for 50 to 60 minutes, or until eggs are set. Cut into squares to serve. Refrigerate leftovers. 8 to 10 servings.

Edie Hamer, Indiana

DRIED BEEF & MACARONI

- 1 tray LORI'S KITCHEN Creamed Chipped Beef, thawed
- 1 cup milk
- 1 cup uncooked elbow macaroni
- 8 slices SCHWAN'S American Processed Cheese, cut into strips

In 1½ to 2-quart casserole, thoroughly mix all ingredients. Cover; refrigerate several hours or overnight.

Heat oven to 350°F. and bake for 35 to 45 minutes. Refrigerate leftovers. 4 to 5 servings.

TIP: For a crusty top, bake uncovered.

By June of 1964 Schwan's had expanded its ice cream selection to over 25 flavors.

Sharon Potucek, New York

EASY CHEESY CREAMED COD

6 pieces SEAFARER'S CHOICE IQF Cod Fillets
1 (16-oz.) tub LORI'S KITCHEN Wisconsin Cheese Deli Soup
½ teaspoon dried basil leaves
½ teaspoon paprika
¼ teaspoon garlic powder
Cooked GOURMET'S CHOICE IQF White Rice, if desired

In 13x9-inch microwave-safe dish, place fillets. Cover; microwave on HIGH for 8 minutes, or until fish flakes easily with a fork. In 2½-quart microwave-safe casserole, place soup; microwave on HIGH for 5 to 6 minutes, or until hot. Add fillets, basil, paprika and garlic powder; stir gently. Cover and microwave on HIGH for 2 to 4 minutes, or until hot. Serve over cooked rice, if desired. Refrigerate leftovers. 4 servings.

NOTE: Microwave timings are for 700 to 800 watt microwave ovens. With an oven of different wattage output, timings may need slight adjustment.

Neva Thomas, Virginia

COD FILLETS BOSTON

6 SEAFARER'S CHOICE Cod Fillets
Salt, to taste
Pepper, to taste
1 (16-oz.) tub LORI'S KITCHEN Boston Clam Chowder Seafood Soup, thawed
4 cups GOURMET'S CHOICE Early Garden Blend
3 slices SCHWAN'S American Processed Cheese
4 to 6 cups cooked GOURMET'S CHOICE IQF White Rice

Heat oven to 375°F. Spray 11x7-inch baking dish with nonstick cooking spray. Place fillets in prepared dish; salt and pepper to taste. Pour soup over fillets. Bake at 375°F. for 20 to 30 minutes.

Meanwhile, cook Early Garden Blend according to package directions; drain. Place vegetables in a shallow dish; lay cheese slices on vegetables. Microwave rice according to package directions. Place cooked rice on serving platter; make a well in center of rice. Spoon vegetables and cheese into well. Place fillets around rice; pour soup over rice. Refrigerate leftovers. 6 servings.

Cod Fillets Boston

$1,000 Winner
Denise Townsend, Washington

MONTEREY COD

- 8 SEAFARER'S CHOICE Cod Fillets IQF, partially thawed
- ¼ cup fresh lemon juice
- ½ teaspoon seasoned salt
- 2 cups shredded Monterey Jack cheese
- 1 cup chopped green onions
- 1 cup sliced fresh mushrooms
- 2 cups diced tomatoes
- ⅛ teaspoon seasoned salt

Heat oven to 500°F. In 13x9-inch pan arrange fillets; pour lemon juice over fillets and sprinkle with ½ teaspoon seasoned salt. Layer over fillets cheese, green onions, mushrooms and tomatoes; sprinkle with ⅛ teaspoon seasoned salt. Cover with foil and bake at 500°F. for 15 minutes or until fish flakes easily with fork. Refrigerate leftovers. 4 servings.

"The desserts are wonderful; we really look forward to the ice cream."
Denise Townsend

Monterey Cod

Marjorie Yoder, Michigan

FISH VERACRUZ

- ½ cup chopped onions
- 1 medium green bell pepper, chopped
- 3 tomatoes, chopped
- 1 to 2 jalapeño peppers, seeded and chopped
- 1½ to 2 tablespoons olive oil or butter
- 1 bay leaf
- ½ teaspoon oregano
- ½ teaspoon chili powder
- ½ teaspoon ground cumin
- 3 to 4 SEAFARER'S CHOICE Blue Hake Prime Cut Loins OR 6 to 8 SEAFARER'S CHOICE IQF Cod Fillets
- Garlic clove, minced
- ¼ cup fresh lime juice

Heat oven to 425°F. In medium (10-inch) skillet, sauté onions, bell peppers, tomatoes and jalapeño peppers in olive oil until onions and peppers are tender. Add bay leaf, oregano, chili powder and cumin; set aside. In 13x9-inch baking dish place fish; sprinkle with garlic and pour lime juice over. Spoon vegetables over fish. Bake, uncovered, at 425°F. for 20 minutes or until fish flakes easily with a fork. Refrigerate leftovers. 6 servings.

VARIATIONS

Grill fish before placing in baking dish, decrease cooking time to 8 to 10 minutes. Gives a grilled Southwest flavor.

½ lb. SEAFARER'S CHOICE P & D Shrimp can be added during the last 4 minutes of baking. When served, top with diced avocados.

Rosilee Butler, North Carolina

HADDOCK BAKE

½ cup butter or margarine
4 to 6 SEAFARER'S CHOICE Haddock Squares
1 (1 lb.) package GOURMET'S CHOICE Breaded Onion Rings
½ (1½ lb.) package GOURMET'S CHOICE Breaded Mushrooms
Fresh chopped parsley
Cooked GOURMET'S CHOICE California Blend, if desired

Heat oven to 400°F. Melt butter in 13x9-inch pan. Lay haddock in single layer; top with onion rings and mushrooms. Bake at 400°F. for 10 minutes; turn over onion rings and mushrooms. Bake additional 10 minutes. Sprinkle with parsley. Serve with California Blend. Refrigerate leftovers. 6 to 8 servings.

Arnita Somerville, Illinois

SEAFOOD BURRITOS

1 SEAFARER'S CHOICE Blue Hake Prime Cut Loin, cooked
1 cup SEAFARER'S CHOICE P & D Shrimp, cooked and cut into thirds
1 cup crab meat, cooked OR 1 (6-oz.) can crab meat
8 slices SCHWAN'S American Processed Cheese
¼ cup salsa
¼ cup dairy sour cream
4 (10-inch) flour tortillas
Dairy sour cream

Cut Blue Hake into bite-size pieces; combine with shrimp and crab. Divide seafood evenly among tortillas. On seafood place a cheese slice; spread with 1 tablespoon salsa and 1 tablespoon sour cream. Roll up. Top with 1 slice of cheese. Place in a 13x9-inch microwave-safe pan; microwave on HIGH for 2 to 3 minutes. Serve with additional sour cream and salsa if desired. Refrigerate leftovers. 4 servings.

NOTE: Microwave timings are for 700 to 800 watt microwave ovens. With an oven of different wattage output, timings may need slight adjustment.

Seafood Burritos

D'Anne Gresham, Texas

EASY FISH DINNER

1 SEAFARER'S CHOICE Orange Roughy Fillet
1 cup GOURMET'S CHOICE Stir-Fry Vegetables or GOURMET'S CHOICE California Blend
3 tablespoons prepared ranch dressing
Salt, to taste
Pepper, to taste

Heat oven to 400°F. On 12-inch square piece of foil, place fillet, vegetables, dressing, salt and pepper; fold securely. Bake at 400°F. for 15 to 20 minutes, or until fish flakes easily with a fork. Refrigerate leftovers. 1 serving.

Delila Webster, South Dakota

FISH CASSEROLE

2 chicken bouillon cubes
2 cups hot water
2 cups GOURMET'S CHOICE IQF White Rice
1 pound GOURMET'S CHOICE Broccoli Spears, chopped
½ teaspoon Italian seasoning
½ teaspoon garlic powder
2 SEAFARER'S CHOICE Blue Hake Prime Cut Loins, thawed
⅛ teaspoon paprika
½ cup shredded Monterey Jack cheese
1 (2.8-oz.) can French-fried onions

Heat oven to 350°F. In measuring cup dissolve bouillon cubes in hot water. In medium bowl, combine bouillon, rice, broccoli, Italian seasoning and garlic powder; mix well. Spoon into 13x9-inch pan; top with fish. Sprinkle with paprika. Bake at 350°F. for 30 minutes or until fish flakes easily with a fork. Top with cheese and onions; bake additional 5 minutes. Refrigerate leftovers. 6 servings.

Fish Casserole

June Stelter, Minnesota

BAKED FISH–EASY!

- ½ large white onion, thinly sliced
- 2 tablespoons butter or margarine
- 1 teaspoon dried dill weed
- 1 teaspoon garlic powder
- ½ teaspoon salt
- ½ teaspoon pepper
- 4 SEAFARER'S CHOICE Blue Hake Prime Cut Loins
- ½ cup bread crumbs OR buttery cracker crumbs
- ½ cup shredded sharp Cheddar cheese
- ¼ cup butter or margarine
- Fresh lemon, if desired

Heat oven to 400°F. In small skillet, sauté onion slices in 2 tablespoons butter; set aside. Spray 13x9-inch pan with nonstick cooking spray. In small bowl, mix dill weed, garlic powder, salt and pepper. Place fish in prepared pan; sprinkle evenly with herb mixture. Layer onions, crumbs and cheese over herbs. Cut butter into small pieces and sprinkle over top. Bake at 400°F. for 15 to 20 minutes, or until fish flakes easily with a fork. Squeeze fresh lemon over fish, if desired. Refrigerate leftovers. 2 to 4 servings.

$1,000 Winner
Ardelle Peka, Minnesota

SOUTH OF THE BORDER FISH BAKE

- 1 pound SEAFARER'S CHOICE Blue Hake Prime Cut Loins
- ½ cup dairy sour cream
- 1 tablespoon lemon juice
- 1 tablespoon milk
- ¾ cup finely crushed corn chips
- 2 tablespoons butter or margarine, melted
- Salsa, if desired
- Shredded cheese, if desired
- Shredded lettuce, if desired

Heat oven to 400°F. Place foil in 13x9-inch baking pan; grease foil, set aside. Cut frozen fish into serving-size pieces. In shallow dish combine sour cream, lemon juice and milk. Dip fish in sour cream mixture and then into chips; place in prepared pan. Drizzle with melted margarine. Bake at 400°F. for 15 to 20 minutes or until fish flakes easily with a fork. Serve topped with salsa, cheese and lettuce, if desired. Refrigerate leftovers. 2 servings.

"I've used it for years. We've been with Schwan's for as long as they've serviced the area."

Ardelle Peka

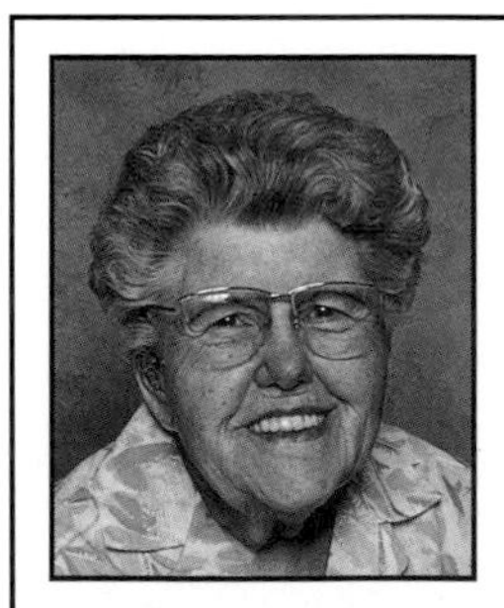

South of the Border Fish Bake

$1,000 Winner
Sue Olson, Georgia

SHRIMP & TORTELLINI

2 cups LORI'S KITCHEN Cheese Tortellini
⅓ cup butter or margarine
5 cups SEAFARER'S CHOICE P & D Shrimp, thawed
2 tablespoons minced green onions
2 teaspoons dried basil leaves
½ cup grated Parmesan cheese
⅛ to ¼ teaspoon freshly ground pepper
Fresh parsley

Cook pasta according to package directions; set aside. Melt butter in medium (10-inch) skillet over medium-high heat; add shrimp, onions and basil. Cook, stirring constantly, for 4 to 5 minutes, or until shrimp are hot. Add pasta, cheese and pepper; toss gently. Garnish with parsley. Refrigerate leftovers. 4 servings.

Shrimp & Tortellini

Schwan's TIP

Q: Can imitation ingredients be used in recipes in place of the real thing?

A: If you wish to use imitation ingredients in cooking, experiment first to be aware of any visual or textural changes to the product. Imitation cheese and imitation chocolate may melt and set up differently from the products they are meant to replace.

Sarah Smith, North Carolina

SWEET & SOUR SHRIMP

2 tablespoons honey
1 tablespoon vinegar
1 garlic clove, minced
2 tablespoons soy sauce
1 tablespoon tomato paste
1/8 or less teaspoon cumin
1 pound SEAFARER'S CHOICE P & D Shrimp
2 tablespoons peanut oil
3 to 4 cups cooked GOURMET'S CHOICE IQF White Rice

In shallow dish, combine honey, vinegar, garlic, soy sauce, tomato paste and cumin; mix well. Add shrimp; stir to coat. Cover; refrigerate 30 minutes, stirring occasionally.

Remove shrimp from marinade. Heat oil in wok or large (12-inch) skillet over high heat; stir-fry shrimp 3 minutes. Add marinade; reduce heat to medium and cook for 2 minutes, or until marinade is hot and shrimp are pink. Serve over rice. Refrigerate leftovers. 4 servings.

Diane Neeley, Missouri

SEAFOOD PASTA

1 pound linguini pasta
1/2 cup butter or margarine
2 tablespoons flour
1/2 cup chicken broth
1 garlic clove, crushed
2 (6 1/2-oz.) cans chopped clams, undrained
4 ounces SEAFARER'S CHOICE Orange Roughy Fillets, cubed
8 ounces SEAFARER'S CHOICE P & D Shrimp
1/4 cup chopped fresh parsley
1/2 teaspoon salt
1/8 teaspoon pepper

Cook pasta *half* as long as directed on package; drain, keep warm. In large saucepan, combine butter, flour, broth and garlic; cook and stir over medium-high heat until butter melts. Add clams with juice, fish and shrimp; bring to a boil. Add partially cooked noodles and heat thoroughly; add salt, pepper and parsley. Refrigerate leftovers. 4 servings.

Diane Davidson, Texas

QUICK SHRIMP DIABLO

1½ pounds SEAFARER'S CHOICE P & D Shrimp
1 (12-oz.) jar thick-style salsa in mild, medium or hot
¾ teaspoon prepared mustard
4 to 5 cups cooked GOURMET'S CHOICE IQF White Rice
Lemon wedges, if desired

In medium saucepan, bring water sufficient to cover shrimp to boil. Add shrimp and boil until shrimp *just start* to turn pink. Chill under cold running water; drain, set aside. In microwave-safe 1½-quart casserole, combine salsa and mustard; mix well. Cover; microwave on HIGH for 3 minutes, stirring once. Add shrimp and microwave on HIGH for 4 to 6 minutes until thoroughly heated, stirring every 2 minutes. Serve over rice with lemon wedges, if desired. Refrigerate leftovers. 5 to 6 servings.

NOTE: Microwave timings are for 700 to 800 watt microwave ovens. With an oven of different wattage output, timings may need slight adjustment.

T.A. Trachsler, Colorado

QUICKIN CAJUN SHRIMP

1 pound SEAFARER'S CHOICE P & D Shrimp
1 teaspoon olive oil
¼ teaspoon red pepper
1 (24-oz.) jar mild picante sauce
¼ teaspoon garlic powder
⅛ teaspoon ground oregano
Salt, to taste
Pepper, to taste
3 to 4 cups cooked GOURMET'S CHOICE IQF White Rice

Prepare shrimp according to package directions; drain, set aside.

In medium saucepan over medium heat, combine olive oil, red pepper and picante sauce; mix well. Stir in garlic powder, oregano, salt, pepper and shrimp. Cook 5 minutes. Serve over rice. Refrigerate leftovers. 4 servings.

A good buy has always been the hallmark of SCHWAN'S delicious ice cream. This advertisement appeared in an April, 1952 issue of the Marshall Independent.

$1,000 Winner
Phyllis Stimson, California

SCHWAN'S SPICY SHRIMP

- ⅓ cup butter or margarine
- 1½ teaspoons crushed garlic
- 1 teaspoon Worcestershire sauce
- 1 teaspoon dried basil leaves, crushed
- ½ teaspoon crushed red pepper
- ½ teaspoon dried oregano leaves, crushed
- ½ teaspoon salt
- ½ teaspoon black pepper
- ¼ teaspoon cayenne pepper
- 1 large tomato, coarsely diced
- 1 to 2 pounds SEAFARER'S CHOICE P & D Shrimp, thawed
- ¼ cup beer, at room temperature
- 3 cups cooked GOURMET'S CHOICE IQF White Rice

Heat butter in large (12-inch) skillet over high heat. Combine garlic, Worcestershire sauce, basil, red pepper, oregano, salt, pepper and cayenne pepper; mix well. Add tomato and shrimp; cook, stirring constantly for 2 minutes. Add beer. Cover; cook 1 minute or until shrimp are pink. Serve over cooked rice. Refrigerate leftovers. 2 to 3 servings.

"As a child growing up in Iowa I loved SCHWAN'S ice cream and it's a real treat to enjoy all these other things out here now."

Phyllis Stimson

Schwan's Spicy Shrimp

Rebecca Davis, Missouri

SPICY BAKED SHRIMP

- 1 to 1½ pounds SEAFARER'S CHOICE P & D Shrimp
- ½ cup olive oil or oil
- 2 tablespoons Cajun or Creole seasoning
- 2 tablespoons lemon juice
- 2 tablespoons chopped parsley
- 1 tablespoon honey
- 1 tablespoon soy sauce
- ⅛ teaspoon cayenne pepper
- 3 to 4 cups cooked GOURMET'S CHOICE IQF White Rice

In 13x9-inch baking dish, combine shrimp, oil, Cajun or Creole seasoning, lemon juice, parsley, honey, soy sauce and cayenne pepper; mix well. Turn shrimp to coat evenly with mixture. Cover; refrigerate 1 hour, stirring occasionally.

Heat oven to 450°F. Bake 10 minutes, or until shrimp are pink, stirring twice. Serve over cooked rice. Refrigerate leftovers. 4 servings.

BREADS, JAMS & JELLIES

Traditionally the mark of a great cook, homemade preserves and breads now appear in faster, creative new recipes that always yield a winner – including our $10,000 Grand Prize recipient, Polish Sandwich Braid.

Polish Sandwich Braid p.138

Polish Sandwich Braid

$10,000 Winner
Jean Olson, Iowa

POLISH SANDWICH BRAID

3 slices HAUGIN'S FARM BRAND Thick Sliced Bacon, cut into ½-inch pieces
⅓ cup chopped onions
1 small garlic clove, minced
2 HAUGIN'S PRIDE Polish Sausages, coarsely chopped
1 cup sauerkraut, well drained
1 tablespoon brown sugar
⅛ teaspoon caraway seed
1 loaf SCHWAN'S White Frozen Bread Dough
¼ cup grated Swiss cheese
1 egg, beaten
Poppyseed

In large skillet (12-inch) over medium-high heat, cook bacon, onions and garlic until bacon is lightly browned, stirring frequently. Reduce heat to medium. Add sausage, sauerkraut, brown sugar and caraway seed. Cook 5 minutes, stirring occasionally; drain, cool.

On lightly floured surface, roll bread dough to 13x10-inch rectangle; place on greased cookie sheet. Spread filling in 3½-inch strip, lengthwise, down center of dough to within ½ inch of filling. Fold strips of dough alternating from side to side, at an angle halfway across filling, with ends of strips slightly overlapping. Brush with egg; sprinkle with poppyseeds. Cover; let rise in warm place, until double, about 30 minutes.

Heat oven to 375°F. Bake 15 minutes, or until golden brown. Refrigerate leftovers. 6 servings.

Debra Renner, Texas

SAUSAGE BREAD

8 HAUGIN'S FARM BRAND Pork Sausage Patties
1 loaf SCHWAN'S White Frozen Bread Dough
2 eggs, beaten
¼ cup grated Parmesan cheese
1 teaspoon Italian herb seasoning
4 slices SCHWAN'S American Processed Cheese
Melted butter

Heat oven to 350°F. In large (12-inch) skillet over medium-high heat, cook sausage 10 to 12 minutes per side, or until brown. Drain on paper towels; crumble. On lightly floured surface, roll dough out to 14x7-inch rectangle. In large bowl, mix sausage, eggs, Parmesan cheese and Italian herb seasoning; spread on dough. Top with cheese slices. Tightly roll from 7-inch side, pinching ends and shaping into loaf. Cut 3 small slits on top. Place seam-side-down, on ungreased baking sheet. Let rise 10 minutes. Bake at 350°F. for 35 to 40 minutes, or until golden brown. Remove from oven and brush with melted butter. Cool 5 minutes before slicing. Refrigerate leftovers. 8 servings.

*TIP: ¼ teaspoon *each* dried oregano leaves, dried marjoram leaves and dried basil leaves and ⅛ teaspoon rubbed dried sage can be substituted for 1 teaspoon Italian herb seasoning.

“*Our family got started on Schwan's because of their ice cream. We raised 5 kids on it... I think that's why they all grew up happy and healthy.*”

Jean Olson
Grand Prize Winner

Norma Baker, Texas

BRANDY PEACH JAM

8 cups frozen GOURMET'S CHOICE Sliced Peaches, thawed, drained and coarsely chopped
2 tablespoons lemon juice
1 cup peach brandy
1 (1.75-oz.) package powdered pectin
5½ cups sugar

In large saucepan, combine peaches, lemon juice and brandy. Cook over medium-high heat 5 minutes, stirring frequently. Stir in pectin; mix well. Bring mixture to rolling boil (a boil that does not stop when stirred). Boil 5 minutes, stirring constantly. Stir in sugar all at once; mix well. Cook 4 to 5 minutes until mixture returns to a full boil, stirring constantly. Boil 1 minute. Remove from heat. Stir 3 minutes to distribute fruit. Pour hot mixture into hot, clean jars, leaving ¼-inch head space. Adjust caps. Process 10 minutes in boiling water bath. 7 to 8 half-pints.

Grace Wangberg, South Dakota

FRUIT LOAF

1 loaf SCHWAN'S White Frozen Bread Dough, thawed
⅓ cup currants
⅓ cup fruit cake mixed fruit
¼ cup slivered almonds
1 packet icing for BRIGHT STARTS Cinnamon Rolls*

Spray 9x5x3-inch loaf pan with nonstick cooking spray. Allow dough to rise (about 2 to 3 hours) until double in size; punch dough down. On lightly floured surface, pat or roll out dough to 10x6-inch rectangle; sprinkle with currants, mixed fruit and almonds. Starting at short side, tightly roll up dough. Place seam-side-down in prepared pan. Cover; let rise until double in size, about 30 minutes.

Heat oven to 350°F. Bake for 30 minutes or until golden brown. Remove from pan; cool on rack. Frost with prepared icing. 1 loaf.

*TIP: To substitute for prepared icing. In small bowl, mix 1 cup powdered sugar and enough milk to make a thin glaze.

Brandy Peach Jam
Cinnamon-Apple Jelly p.142
Fruit Loaf

Sharen Green, Maryland

CINNAMON-APPLE JELLY

1 quart prepared VITA-SUN Apple Juice Drink Concentrate
1 (1.75-oz.) package powdered pectin
4½ cups sugar
3 tablespoons cinnamon candies

In large saucepan, combine juice and powdered pectin; mix well. Bring to a full rolling boil (a boil that does not stop when stirred) over medium heat, stirring frequently. Boil 1 minute. Add sugar and candies. Cook until mixture comes to a rolling boil, stirring frequently. Boil 2 minutes. Remove from heat, skim off foam if necessary. Pour hot mixture into clean, hot jars, leaving ¼-inch head space. Cool; seal and freeze. 7 half-pints.

Schwan's TIP

Q: Can liquid and powdered pectins be used interchangeably?

A: No. Be sure to use the type of pectin called for in a recipe, because methods and proportion of ingredients needed may differ with each type of pectin.

Leotta Spooner, Michigan

HOT APPLE BREAKFAST ROLLS

1 tablespoon butter
3 cups (3 medium) granny smith apples, cored, peeled and finely diced
3 tablespoons brown sugar
1 tablespoon lemon juice
1 teaspoon cinnamon
½ teaspoon ginger
½ teaspoon cloves
½ cup chopped walnuts
½ cup raisins
1 loaf SCHWAN'S White OR SCHWAN'S Honey Wheat Frozen Bread Dough, thawed

GLAZE

½ cup powdered sugar
3 to 4 tablespoons lemon juice

Heat oven to 350°F. Grease a 13x9-inch pan; set aside. Melt butter in large (12-inch) skillet over medium heat. Add apples, brown sugar, lemon juice, cinnamon, ginger and cloves; sauté for 3 minutes, or until apples are tender, stirring occasionally. Remove from heat; add nuts and raisins; cool. On lightly floured surface, roll dough out to 15x10¼-inch rectangle; spread with apple mixture. Starting at short side, roll up tightly; cut into 18 equal pieces. Place cut-side-down in prepared pan. Cover; let rise in warm place until double in size, about 20 to 30 minutes. Bake at 350°F. for 30 to 35 minutes, or until golden brown.

Meanwhile, in small bowl, combine all glaze ingredients; mix well to dissolve sugar. Spoon glaze over warm rolls. 18 rolls.

TIP: For a sweeter roll, glaze can be doubled.

Alice Brekke, North Dakota

BROCCOLI ROLLS

- 1 loaf SCHWAN'S White Frozen Bread Dough, thawed
- ½ pound GOURMET'S CHOICE Broccoli Spears
- ½ cup ricotta cheese
- 1 egg
- 1 cup mozzarella cheese
- 3 tablespoons butter, melted
- 1 tablespoon garlic powder
- ½ teaspoon dried oregano leaves

Grease 15x10-inch pan. On lightly floured surface, divide dough into 4 equal parts. Roll each part out to 9x5x¼-inch rectangle. In medium saucepan, cook broccoli in 1 inch of boiling water for 3 minutes. Drain by squeezing with paper towels; cut into 1-inch pieces.

In small bowl, combine ricotta cheese and egg; mix well. Spread ¼ of ricotta mixture, ¼ of broccoli pieces and ¼ cup of mozzarella cheese on half of each dough piece. Fold other half of dough over filling; pinch edges to seal. Place rolls on prepared pan. Brush tops with butter; sprinkle with garlic powder and oregano. Let rise in warm place until double in size, about 20 minutes. Heat oven to 400°F. Bake 15 to 20 minutes, or until golden brown. Refrigerate leftovers. 4 rolls.

Connie Coffey, Missouri

BROCCOLI CHEESE BREAD

- 6 to 8 (1 lb.) HAUGIN'S FARM BRAND Pork Sausage Patties
- ½ package (1 lb.) GOURMET'S CHOICE Broccoli Spears
- 1 loaf SCHWAN'S White Frozen Bread Dough, thawed
- 4 cups shredded mozzarella cheese

In large skillet (12-inch) over medium heat cook and crumble sausage until well browned; drain well. Prepare broccoli according to package directions; drain, cut into bite-size pieces.

Heat oven to 350°F. On lightly floured surface, roll out dough to 20x14-inch rectangle. Layer cheese, sausage and broccoli in a 4-inch strip lengthwise down center of dough. Fold sides over filling, pinching edges and ends to seal. Place seam-side-down, folding ends under, on *ungreased* cookie sheet. Bake at 350°F. for 25 to 30 minutes, or until golden brown. Refrigerate leftovers. 6 servings.

D'Et Otis, Montana

POTATO BUNS

1 loaf SCHWAN'S White Frozen Bread Dough, thawed
6 large potatoes, peeled, cut into sixths
½ teaspoon onion salt
½ teaspoon pepper
½ cup butter
½ cup chopped onions
Garlic salt
Dairy sour cream

In large saucepan over medium-high heat, heat 1 inch of water to boiling. Add potatoes. Bring water to boil. Cover; reduce heat to low. Cook 20 minutes, or until tender. Drain; mash until smooth. Add onion salt and pepper; set aside.

Cut dough into 16 equal pieces. Flatten each to 2½ to 3-inch diameter circle. Place about ⅓-cup potato mixture on dough. Bring all edges together, pinching to seal and shaping into a ball. Place seam-side-down, ½ inch apart on greased cookie sheets. Cover; let rise in warm place until double in size, about 30 to 40 minutes.

Heat oven to 375°F. Bake for 15 to 20 minutes, or until golden brown.

Meanwhile, melt butter in small skillet over medium-high heat; sauté onions 5 to 6 minutes, or until light brown. Place hot baked buns in large pan or bowl. Pour onion mixture over rolls; shake gently to coat. Cover with towel; let stand 15 minutes. Serve warm with garlic salt and sour cream. 16 buns.

Potato Buns

Carole Belcher, Tennessee

ROSEMARY-ONION BREAD

5 tablespoons olive oil, divided
1 loaf SCHWAN'S White Frozen Bread Dough, thawed
½ cup grated Parmesan cheese
1 medium onion, thinly sliced and separated into rings
1 tablespoon chopped fresh rosemary or 1½ teaspoons dried rosemary, crushed
1 teaspoon salt
Grated Parmesan cheese

Heat oven to 375°F. Lightly coat a 17x11-inch cookie sheet with 1 teaspoon oil. Pat or roll out dough to 16x11-inch rectangle. Brush dough with 4 tablespoons of the olive oil. Sprinkle with cheese and onion rings, pressing onion rings lightly into dough. Cover with plastic wrap; allow to rise in warm place until double in size, about 1 hour. Drizzle 2 teaspoons olive oil over onions; sprinkle with rosemary and salt.

Bake at 375°F. for 15 to 20 minutes. Sprinkle with Parmesan cheese, if desired; serve warm. 6 servings.

Sharon Buchler, Michigan

PEACH STREUSEL COFFEE CAKE

STREUSEL TOPPING
½ cup all-purpose flour
¼ cup butter or margarine
¼ cup firmly packed brown sugar
1 teaspoon vanilla
Chopped nuts, if desired

COFFEE CAKE
1 loaf SCHWAN'S White OR SCHWAN'S Honey Wheat Frozen Bread Dough, thawed
1 pound (about ½ pkg.) GOURMET'S CHOICE Sliced Peaches, thawed and *well drained*

Heat oven to 350°F. Lightly spoon flour into measuring cup; level off. In small bowl, combine flour and butter. Using pastry blender or fork, cut in butter until mixture resembles fine crumbs. Add brown sugar and vanilla; mix well. Stir in nuts, if desired. Pat or roll out dough to fit a greased 13-inch pizza pan. Place peaches on dough; sprinkle with streusel topping.

Bake at 350°F. for 25 to 30 minutes, or until crust is golden brown. 10 to 12 servings.

Paula Curtis, Pennsylvania

MEAT & VEGGIE STROMBOLI

3 loaves SCHWAN'S White Frozen Bread Dough, thawed
1 pound HAUGIN'S FARM BRAND Ham, thinly sliced
1 pound HAUGIN'S PRIDE Summer Sausage, very thinly sliced
4 cups GOURMET'S CHOICE California Blend, thawed
3 cups shredded mozzarella cheese
1 (16-oz.) jar prepared spaghetti sauce

Heat oven to 350°F. Roll out each loaf of bread to a 14x7-inch rectangle. On each rectangle layer ⅓ of the ham, summer sausage, California Blend and mozzarella cheese. Tightly roll from 7-inch side, pinching ends and shaping into loaf. Place seam-side-down on greased cookie sheet. Let rise 10 minutes. Bake at 350°F. for 25 to 30 minutes, or until golden brown.

In small saucepan, heat spaghetti sauce until hot. Cut stromboli in slices; serve with sauce. Refrigerate leftovers. 8 to 10 servings.

Meat & Veggie Stromboli

Strawberry

Karen Gonzales, Arizona

GAME DAY BARBEQUE SANDWICHES

1 loaf SCHWAN'S White Frozen Bread Dough, thawed
1 (1½-lb.) package HAUGIN'S PRIDE Chopped BBQ Beef with Sauce, thawed
4 small onions, thinly sliced
4 slices SCHWAN'S American Processed Cheese
1 tablespoon butter or margarine, melted
½ cup crushed canned French-fried onion rings

Heat oven to 350°F. On lightly floured surface, divide dough into 4 equal pieces. Roll each into 10-inch circle. Top half of each with ¼ of barbecued beef, ¼ of the onion slices and 1 slice of cheese. Fold half of dough over filling, pinching edges to seal. Brush with melted butter; top with onion rings. Cover with plastic wrap; let rise for 20 minutes. Bake at 350°F. for 20 to 25 minutes, or until golden brown. Remove from oven; let stand for 5 minutes before serving. Refrigerate leftovers. 4 servings.

Game Day Barbeque Sandwiches
Schwan's "Super Bowl" Snack p.17

Karen Gonzales, Arizona

HOT CLUB SUB

8 slices HAUGIN'S FARM BRAND Thick Sliced Bacon
2 loaves SCHWAN'S White Frozen Bread Dough, thawed
¼ cup dijon style mustard
8 ounces HAUGIN'S FARM BRAND Ham, thinly sliced
1 small onion, sliced
½ green bell pepper, thinly sliced
1 cup SCHWAN'S Diced Chicken Meat, thawed
8 slices SCHWAN'S American Processed Cheese
1 to 2 tablespoons butter or margarine, melted
1 tablespoon sesame seeds

Cook bacon in large (12-inch) skillet over medium-high heat until crisp. Drain; crumble, set aside. On lightly floured surface, overlap one long edge of each piece of dough; pinch together. Roll into 18x8-inch rectangle; spread with mustard. Top one half of dough with bacon, ham, onions, pepper, chicken and cheese. Fold other half over; pinch edges to seal. Place on ungreased cookie sheet. Brush with butter; sprinkle with sesame seeds. Cover with plastic wrap and let rise for 20 minutes.

Heat oven to 350°F. Bake for 30 to 35 minutes, or until golden brown. Remove from oven and let stand 5 minutes before serving. Refrigerate leftovers. 10 servings.

DESSERTS

No meal is complete without dessert, whether it's a light Berry Sorbet or a substantial Caramel Blueberry Bread Pudding. Send them away from the table satisfied.

Berry Sorbet p.152